Jeremiah

Christine Lung 2013

*Not yet published as of this printing.

BIBLE STUDY COMMENTARY

Jeremiah

F. B. HUEY, JR.

Lamplighter Books Grand Rapids, Michigan
Zondervan Publishing House

JEREMIAH: BIBLE STUDY COMMENTARY
Copyright © 1981 by The Zondervan Corporation
Grand Rapids, Michigan

Lamplighter Books are published by
Zondervan Publishing House
1415 Lake Drive, S.E.,
Grand Rapids, Michigan 49506

Library of Congress Cataloging in Publication Data

Huey, F. B., 1925-
  Jeremiah, Bible study commentary.

  (Bible study series)
      1. Bible.   O.T.   Jeremiah—Commentaries.   I. Bible.
  O.T.   Jeremiah.   English.   1981.   II. Title.   III. Series.
  BS1525.3.H83   224'.2077   81-1469
  ISBN 0-310-36063-3   AACR2

Edited by John Danilson and Edward Viening

Printed in the United States of America

87 88 89 90 91 92 93 / EP / 11 10 9 8 7 6 5 4

Contents

Introduction

There is no area of Old Testament study more fascinating than that of the prophets and none among them more intriguing than the prophet Jeremiah. He was sensitive, compassionate, uncompromising, and courageous. He was also introspective, lonely, and given to alternating moods of exaltation and despair. Though known as the "weeping prophet," his tears were not symptoms of weakness but of concern for his people.[1]

The Jewish people included him among the Major Prophets in their Scriptures; and, in fact, the book bearing his name is the longest book in the Old Testament. The importance of Jeremiah, however, lies not in the length of the book but in its content. Jeremiah's messages speak to the present age as pointedly as they did to his world.

A. Jeremiah the Man

Jeremiah is the most "human" of all the prophets and the one with whom most people can easily identify. He does not appear to be as majestic as Isaiah, as remote as Ezekiel, or as fearsome as Amos. He reveals his personal feelings and his own struggles with God's claim on his life as does no other prophet. When he was personally attacked, his response was very human—he called on God to bring vengeance on his enemies! But when threatened by death on more than one occasion, he did not flee from his persecutors.

---

[1]The word "jeremiad," a lament, has come into the English language as a reminder of the association of Jeremiah with weeping. However, in Jeremiah's own time he must have earned an impressive reputation for courage and strength, as centuries later people made comparisons between Jesus and Jeremiah (Matt. 16:14).

Jeremiah was called to be a prophet in "the thirteenth year of the reign of Josiah" (1:2; i.e., 627 B.C.). He was probably a young man when called; so the date of his birth was around 650–645 B.C. He was the son of Hilkiah, a priest at Anathoth in the land of Benjamin; he may himself have been a priest, though he never mentions it. It is not likely that his father was the Hilkiah who found the Book of the Law in the temple (2 Kings 22:8). The name Jeremiah has been understood to mean "the Lord hurls," "the Lord loosens," "the Lord exalts," or "the Lord establishes."

Jeremiah seems to have been well off financially, as he had money to purchase the land of a kinsman; and no mention is made of secular work in which he may have been engaged. He was a contemporary of Ezekiel, Daniel, Nahum, Habakkuk, and Zephaniah, though he never mentioned them. He never married (16:1–4).

His ministry may be divided into four periods: (1) from his call to the death of King Josiah, 627–609; (2) from Josiah's death to the deportation of King Jehoiachin, 609–597; (3) during the reign of King Zedekiah, Jehoiachin's successor, until the fall of Jerusalem, 597–587; and (4) after the fall of Jerusalem, including his involuntary flight to Egypt. The story ends in Egypt; whether he ever returned to Jerusalem and when he died cannot be determined.

By human standards Jeremiah would be considered a failure. He preached for more than forty years, and practically no one listened to him. He was rejected by his people, hated, ridiculed, and subjected to persecution. He was unable to avert the destruction of Judah in spite of his impassioned warnings. However, by God's standards he was successful because God required only that Jeremiah obey Him by proclaiming His messages. An obedient servant of the Lord is not held accountable for the lack of response from those who hear him. The kingdoms of Asshurbanipal, Neco, and Nebuchadnezzar (the Napoleons and Hitlers of their day) have vanished. Their names have been forgotten, but the name and influence of Jeremiah still remain.

B. The Times

The Book of Jeremiah cannot be fully understood apart from a knowledge of the times in which he lived. It was a period of unprecedented political upheaval in the ancient Near East. In 609 B.C. Jeremiah witnessed the fall of one of the greatest empires of the ancient world, Assyria, and the rise of its successor, Babylonia. He observed the unsuccessful attempt of Egypt to defeat Babylonia at the battle of Carchemish in 605 that forced her to settle for second place in the hierarchy of nations. Jeremiah was also an eyewitness to the destruction of Jerusalem by the Babylonian armies that ended Judah's political independence. That era has truly been called a time of crisis and transition.

The following chronology will serve the reader as a useful reference throughout the study of the Book of Jeremiah. Dates may vary slightly, depending on the source followed.

B.C.

ca. 650	Birth of Jeremiah during the reign of Manasseh
642–40	Reign of Amon over Judah
640	Beginning of reign of Josiah over Judah *13 yr of Josiah*
627	Call of Jeremiah
626	Babylonia's independence from Assyria established
622	Law book found during Josiah's repairs of the temple
612	Fall of Nineveh to the Medes and Babylonians and effectual end of the Assyrian empire
609	Final collapse of Assyrian resistance. Battle of Megiddo in which Josiah was killed. Reign of Jehoahaz (Shallum) over Judah for three months and beginning of reign of Jehoiakim (Eliakim)
605	Battle of Carchemish with Egypt that established Babylonian supremacy. Nebuchadnezzar became king of Babylonia.
601	Jehoiakim's rebellion against Nebuchadnezzar
598	Death of Jehoiakim and beginning of reign of his son Jehoiachin (Jeconiah/Coniah)
597	Jehoiachin deposed by Nebuchadnezzar after a three-months' reign and taken into exile. Beginning of reign of his uncle Zedekiah (Mattaniah)
587	Destruction of Jerusalem, end of the kingdom of Judah, and deportation of some of its inhabitants. Gedaliah appointed as governor and murdered after a rule of undetermined length. Jeremiah taken to Egypt
582	Another deportation of some inhabitants of Judah
561	Release of Jehoiachin from Babylonian imprisonment
539	Defeat of Babylonia by the Persians

C. The Book

For centuries no serious questions were raised about the genuineness of Jeremianic authorship of the book that bears his name. It was not until 1901 that Bernard Duhm opened the critical attack on Jeremiah by suggesting that Jeremiah only wrote certain poetic portions of the book and the letter in chapter 29.

Duhm's theory has been refined by other scholars so that today critical scholars see at least three major sources in the book: the actual prophetic sayings of Jeremiah that can be identified by their poetic meter, the biographical prose narratives (probably recorded by Baruch or an unknown biographer), and the prose speeches recorded by disciples of Jeremiah or by otherwise unknown Deuteronomic redactors. Conservative scholars argue that the inability of liberal scholars to agree in their analysis of the sources serves as evidence that the unity of the book can still be defended.[2]

The basis for the arrangement of the messages in the book remains an unsolved puzzle. Since it begins with the call of Jeremiah and ends with the destruction of Jerusalem and subsequent events in Egypt, the casual reader may assume that the entire book is arranged chronologically. However, this initial impression quickly proves to be erroneous. For example, chapter 21 describes events in the reign of Zedekiah (597–587), whereas chapter 25 takes place in the reign of Jehoiakim (609–598). Chapters 32–34 are during the reign of Zedekiah, but chapters 35–36 return to events in the reign of Jehoiakim. Therefore, it must be admitted that chronology is only one factor in the arrangement of the book.

---

[2]For a representative critical analysis of the different sources in Jeremiah, see Otto Eissfeldt, *The Old Testament: An Introduction* (New York: Harper & Row, 1965), pp. 350–65. For a defense of Jeremianic authorship see Gleason L. Archer, Jr., *A Survey of Old Testament Introduction*, rev. ed. (Chicago: Moody Press, 1974), pp. 361–62. R. K. Harrison, *Introduction to the Old Testament* (Grand Rapids: Eerdmans, 1969), p. 815, after an extensive history of critical analysis of Jeremiah that makes it evident critical scholars do not agree in their analysis of the book, says that "the process of transmission of the oracles from the lips of the prophet to the ultimate form of the prophecy itself was considerably less complex than has been assumed by the majority of liberal writers on the subject."

It is well to remember an observation by John Calvin concerning the debate over authorship of certain books of the Bible: "Men have not invented what is contained in the Old and New Testaments . . . God is the real author." With an affirmation that the Book of Jeremiah was written under the inspiration of the Spirit of God, disputes among scholars concerning the identity of separate sources become largely academic. Therefore, this commentary will not deal with conjectures about primary and secondary material but will approach the text in its present form to try to understand its meaning and contemporary relevance.

Some sections seem to be grouped together according to subject matter, e.g., the messages against foreign nations, chapters 46–51. Others are arranged according to key words, e.g., the frequent use of "return" in chapters 3–4.

The text followed in our English Bibles differs considerably from the Septuagint version, which is about 2,700 words shorter. The differences are accounted for by omission of single verses or parts of verses. Also the messages against foreign nations (chapters 46–51) are placed after 25:13a in the Septuagint and arranged in a different order.

The style of the book is characterized by the use of a variety of literary forms, e.g., prose, poetry, biography, laments, oracles, and sermons. Frequent repetition of certain words and verses is also characteristic of Jeremiah's style.[3]

D. Outline of the Book

The book is usually divided into three major sections (chapters 1–25, 26–45, 46–51) with chapter 52 serving as a historical postscript. The outline followed in this study, including both major divisions and subdivisions, is incorporated into the text itself as chapter and paragraph headings.

Part One: Messages of Warning to a Disobedient People (1:1–25:38)
  I. The Early Ministry of Jeremiah (1:1–6:30)
    A. Induction into the prophetic office (1:1–19)
      1. Introduction (1:1–3)
      2. Jeremiah's call (1:4–10)   5 = god set him aside for ministry
      3. Vision of an almond branch (1:11–12)
      4. Vision of a boiling pot (1:13–16)
      5. Assurance of strength for the task (1:17–19) 5. strong like iron pillar /wall
    B. Rebuke of Judah's faithlessness to God (2:1–37)
      1. The exchange of God for other deities (2:1–13) not to pray for Judah
      2. Consequences of Judah's faithlessness (2:14–19)
      3. Unrestrained attraction to idolatry (2:20–28)
      4. Judah's refusal to acknowledge her guilt (2:29–37)
    C. A plea to return to God (3:1–4:4)
      1. Judah as the unfaithful wife (3:1–5)
      2. A comparison of guilt (3:6–11)

[3]See S. R. Driver, *An Introduction to the Literature of the Old Testament* (New York: Meridian Books, 1956 reprint), pp. 275–77, for a list of repetitions in Jeremiah.

  – rebellent Lord
  – replace god ē idol
        living H₂O ē broken cistern

God remember Israel

Rom 3:4

PART ONE: *Messages of Warning to a Disobedient People*

Chapter 1

The Early Ministry of Jeremiah
(Jeremiah 1:1–6:30)

The story of Jeremiah begins with his call to be a prophet. Nothing is known about his childhood, family life, education, or other influences on his formative years. However, nothing that happened or that would happen to him could be quite so significant as God's call to the young man from Anathoth. It changed the direction of his life and influenced all that he did until the end of his days.

A. Induction Into the Prophetic Office (1:1–19)

1. Introduction (1:1–3)

The first three verses tell all that is known about the family of Jeremiah and establish the dates of his ministry. Though it is not clear whether Jeremiah himself was a priest, we do know that he was from a family of priests and was the son of Hilkiah (1:1). He was probably a descendant of David's priest, Abiathar, who was banished to Anathoth by Solomon (1 Kings 2:26). Anathoth was four miles northeast of Jerusalem in the territory of the tribe of Benjamin.

However one understands the process of revelation, the Book of Jeremiah affirms repeatedly that God speaks. The first chapter uses three principal expressions of divine communication to which Jeremiah continually referred: (1) "the word of the LORD came to" (literally, "was to," "suggesting that God's word exists); (2) "the Lord said,"; and (3) "declares the Lord"[1] ("saith the Lord," KJV; the verb suggests whispering in the ear, a most intimate revelation). He began hearing God's messages in the thirteenth year of Josiah's reign (1:2, i.e., 627 B.C.). He

---

[1]Unless otherwise indicated, the New International Version is the text quoted throughout this book.

continued hearing the word until after the fall of Jerusalem in 587, a ministry that spanned more than forty years.

2. Jeremiah's call (1:4-10)

A study of the calls of the prophets reveals that no two were exactly alike. Each call was initiated by God, and each one confronted the prophet with the compulsion to accept or the freedom to reject the call, and gave a new direction to his life.[2] Jeremiah sometimes questioned things that happened to him, but he never questioned the genuineness of his call.

However one interprets the doctrine of predestination, it is clear that God told Jeremiah he had been set apart for a prophetic ministry even before his birth[3] (cf. Isa. 49:1, 5; Gal. 1:15). "I formed you" is the same verb used of the potter who shapes clay (18:4; cf. Gen. 2:7). "I knew you" (1:5) suggests that God had complete knowledge of Jeremiah. "I set you apart" (1:5; "I sanctified," KJV; "I consecrated," NASB) comes from a word that means "to separate." It is the same word that means "holy." The form of the verb means that the act of separation had already been completed by God.

Jeremiah's response to being told that he was to be a "prophet to the nations" was anything but enthusiastic. His attempt to excuse himself by insisting, "I do not know how to speak" (1:6), echoes Moses' excuse when God called him from the burning bush (Exod. 4:10). Jeremiah added that he was only a "child." The word can be used of an infant (Exod. 2:6), a child (1 Sam. 2:11), a young man (2 Sam. 18:5), or even a person about middle age (Exod. 33:11). Here it probably refers to inexperience rather than to Jeremiah's actual age.

The Lord refused to accept his excuses but insisted that he "must go to everyone I send you to and say whatever I command you" (1:7). There was no need to be afraid because he had the promise of God's presence with him (1:8).[4]

Then by touching Jeremiah's mouth, the Lord showed symbolically that His words had been put in the prophet's mouth. Similarly, Isaiah's

---

[2]A study of the calls of the prophets can be quite profitable. Compare the calls of Moses (Exod. 3-4), Samuel (1 Sam. 3), Elisha (1 Kings 19:19-21), Amos (Amos 7:14-15), Isaiah (Isa. 6), and Ezekiel (Ezek. 1) for their similarities and differences.

[3]The statement has relevance for the contemporary debate about the morality of abortion.

[4]Study elsewhere in the Bible the use of the phrases "Do not be afraid" (e.g., Gen. 15:1; Num. 21:34; Dan. 10:12; Luke 1:30; Acts 27:24) and "I am (or will be) with you" (e.g., Gen. 28:15; Exod. 3:12; Josh. 1:5; Judg. 6:16; Hag. 1:13; Matt. 28:20).

mouth was touched with a burning coal to symbolize cleansing (Isa. 6:6–7). Ezekiel was given a scroll to eat, signifying complete identification with God's words (Ezek. 2:8–3:3). For Jeremiah, who felt inadequate for the task, the gesture symbolized empowerment. In each case the prophet received what he needed to become a fit spokesman for the Lord.

Jeremiah's ministry would be both destructive and constructive: "to uproot and tear down, to destroy and overthrow, to build and to plant" (1:10; cf. Eccl. 3:1–3). Jeremiah's messages would emphasize both judgment and renewal. The order was correct. Before there could be reconstruction and fruitfulness in Israel, there had to be purging and removal of idolatry and other sins that were keeping the Israelites from being the people of God they were supposed to be. It is always easy to criticize and destroy institutions and beliefs. However, those who do so frequently have nothing constructive to offer as alternatives. The context suggests that the secret of power in Jeremiah's ministry would be God's Word, not Jeremiah's cleverness or ability.

3. Vision of an almond branch (1:11–12)

Jeremiah's call was followed by two visions whose purpose seemed to be to reinforce or confirm his call. Whether they occurred immediately after the call or sometime later cannot be determined. The exact nature and time of each vision is uncertain, but all visions here and elsewhere in the Old Testament are accompanied by spoken words.

The key to understanding the first vision is found in a play on words, a device used frequently by the prophets (e.g., Amos 8:2). Jeremiah was shown a branch of an almond tree (*shaqed*), followed by God's declaration that He was watching (*shoqed*) over His word to fulfill it. *Shaqed* is not the usual word for almond tree. It means "to be awake/watchful" and is used here in recognition of the early blossoming of the almond in the spring while other trees are still in their winter dormancy. Even as the almond blooms early in the spring, the word play suggests that God was awake and alert to the evil in Judah and was preparing to send judgment. He was not unaware of or asleep to Judah's sins. The vision should not be interpreted to mean God was watching over Judah with tender, protective care.

4. Vision of a boiling pot (1:13–16)

Jeremiah was shown a boiling pot (1:13; literally, "a pot blown upon") on the fire, tilted slightly to the south, with its contents about to spill over. The meaning of the vision was clear. Judah was about to be engulfed by an enemy who would approach from the north. The identification of this enemy as Scythians has been generally abandoned by scholars. Disaster from the north would not be incompatible with Babylon as the instrument of judgment, though geographically it lay to the east of Judah. An invading army would not come directly across the forbidding Arabian desert but would follow the Euphrates River, thereby entering Judah by way of Syria to the north. The punishment was justified because of Judah's faithlessness (1:16). The people were worshiping idols made with their own hands.

5. Assurance of strength for the task (1:17-19)

God encouraged Jeremiah to prepare himself for the violent reaction of his own people to his messages. He said, "Get yourself ready!" (1:17). The Hebrew idiom is reproduced in the KJV as "Gird up thy loins," for which a contemporary equivalent could be "Roll up your sleeves!" Jeremiah was not to be "terrified" (1:17; "dismayed," KJV; literally, "shattered") by their response, lest God terrify him before them.

Like a fortified city God would keep him secure. Like an iron pillar and a bronze wall he would be strong enough to resist any attack directed against him (1:18; cf. Ezek. 3:9). What Jeremiah would need was a "thick skin"! The figures of 1:18 are defensive in nature; apparently his only offensive weapon would be the words placed in his mouth (cf. Eph. 6:17). Jeremiah's confidence was to be found in the promise: "I am with you" (1:19). Again the prophet was reminded of God's abiding presence with him (cf. 1:8).

B. Rebuke of Judah's Faithlessness to God (2:1-37)

In this chapter God severely rebuked His people for their faithlessness. At the same time He reminded them of His faithfulness. He challenged them to accuse Him of any failure on His part that would justify their fickleness.

1. The exchange of God for other deities (2:1-13)

God commanded Jeremiah, "Go and proclaim in the hearing of Jerusalem" (2:1) and then added the actual message the prophet was to convey. Although omitted in the NIV, the Hebrew text begins the quoted message in 2:1 with the words "Thus says the LORD" (NASB, RSV).[5] There is no reason to doubt that Jeremiah began preaching soon after his call. The oracles in 2:1–6:30 are generally conceded to have been delivered during the reign of King Josiah. They therefore represent Jeremiah's earliest preaching.

As a warning to Jerusalem, the Lord recalled the years in the desert in idealistic terms (as does Hos. 2:15; but see Ezek. 20:13 for a different picture, one of a rebellious people in the desert). He recalled their earlier "devotion" (2:2), a word that describes covenant loyalty. The desert was a "land not sown" (2:2), i.e., Israel did not plant crops but depended on manna for food. Israel was the "firstfruits of his harvest" (2:3; cf. Lev. 23:10–14, 17; Deut. 26:1–11; James 1:18). Thus anyone who harmed God's people would experience His wrath.

In 2:4–8 we find courtroom language. Making Himself the defendant, God challenged the "house of Jacob" (found twenty times in the Old Testament for the more usual "house of Israel" [cf. Gen. 32:28]) to make accusations against Him that would justify their faithlessness (2:4–5). Though He had brought them into a fruitful land, they showed no gratitude or remembrance of Him but defiled the land by their sins (2:6–7). The leaders were neglecting their responsibilities and leading the people astray. The priests did not seek the Lord; those who dealt with the law did not even know Him. Their rulers (literally, "shepherds," a frequent designation of rulers in the ancient Near East [see Ezek. 34]) rebelled against God, and the prophets prophesied by Baal (2:8).

The courtroom imagery continues in 2:9–11, but in these verses God assumed the role of prosecutor instead of defendant. He charged that other nations did not change their gods, even though they were not really gods, but Israel did! She abandoned her glorious God for "worthless idols" (2:11; literally, "without use/advantage"). Even the created order ("heavens," 2:12) was horrified by the two evils committed by Israel: (1) they have forsaken God, who is the source of living

---

[5]The phrase "Thus says the LORD," which frequently introduces Jeremiah's messages, is called "the messenger formula" because it is similar to words used by messengers of kings in the ancient Near East. These men were sent to various parts of the kingdom to proclaim the edicts of their rulers. To establish the authority of the decree, the messenger would stand before his audience and proclaim, "Thus says the king of . . . ," and the people would listen in respectful silence (2 Kings 18:19; 2 Chron. 18:26; 32:10). When the prophets announced, "Thus says the LORD," their audiences understood they were claiming the authority of their Ruler, the Lord Himself, for what they were about to say.

water (cf. John 4:10–14); (2) they have replaced Him with worthless substitutes. Their gods are compared to cracked cisterns that are unable to hold water (2:13; the porous limestone rock of Palestine was lined with plaster to hold water, especially for the hot, dry summers). The people of Judah were committing the sin that had destroyed Israel: they were embracing worthless substitutes for God.

2. *Consequences of Judah's faithlessness* (2:14–19)

A person could become a slave in the ancient world through capture in wartime, by purchase, for nonpayment of debts, or by birth to slave parents ("homeborn," 2:14 KJV; cf. Exod. 21:4; Lev. 25:54). Israel was none of these; yet she was being victimized, like the prey of lions (2:15; probably a reference to Assyria), or like a slave whose head is "shaved" (2:16; literally, "grazed" or "pastured"; "broken," KJV, by changing the Hebrew vowels). The men of Memphis (literally, Noph, the ancient capital of lower Egypt) and Tahpanhes (modern Tel Defneh in northeastern Egypt) represent past Egyptian humiliation of Israel.

The answer to the question in 2:14 is found in verse 17: Israel brought calamity on herself by forsaking God. Jeremiah warned that it was useless to turn to Egypt for help (2:18; "to drink water from the Shihor," i.e., a branch of the Nile; the word means "black" or "dark" and refers to the color of the water). It was equally futile to turn to Assyria for help (2:18; "to drink water from the River," i.e., the Euphrates). Sin always bears within it the seeds of punishment; Judah's wickedness would bring its own punishment (2:19).

3. *Unrestrained attraction to idolatry* (2:20–28)

To make quite clear the seriousness of Judah's sin, the prophet in 2:20–24 employs six metaphors to show Judah's faithlessness. First, she was like an ox whose yoke is broken (2:20); unyoked, an ox cannot be put to useful service. Where the NIV reads "You broke off your yoke," the Hebrew says, "I broke your yoke" (NASB). There is no need here to change the pronoun "I" to "You," as the reference is to Egyptian bondage that was broken by God.

In spite of the freedom that God gave Israel, she refused to serve Him. Though claiming to be free, she had enslaved herself to the Canaanite fertility deities, like a harlot.

The prophet then compared Judah to a choice vine (2:21; literally, *soreq*, the name of a particular kind of grape of excellent quality). The divine Owner had planted good stock (the stock of the seed of Abraham), but Judah was like a vine that reverted to the wild state (cf. Isa. 5:1–7; Ezek. 17:5–10).

Judah was next described as having an indelible stain that could not be removed by the most vigorous scrubbing or by the strongest soap (2:22). Though her guilt was apparent, the people refused to admit it (2:23). One would only have to look in the valley (probably the Valley of Ben Hinnom; cf. 7:31) to see the evidences of their idolatrous practices that included human sacrifice.

Next, Judah was compared to a swift she-camel and then to a wild donkey (2:23–24). The she-camel is pictured as having no driver, running here and there with no sense of purpose. The wild donkey is described in rather blunt language as an animal in heat at mating time. Just so, Judah had passionately and eagerly sought out idols, like an animal consumed by physical lust. In an ironic appeal God warned them not to continue pursuing their idols until their shoes wore out or their throats were parched with thirst. But a nation who had insisted it would not serve the true God (2:20) now acknowledged its bondage to its idols: "It's no use! I love foreign gods, and I must go after them" (2:25).

The foolishness of idol worship is forcefully expressed in 2:26–28 (cf. also 10:1–16). Kings, officials, priests, and prophets together had been exposed like a thief caught in the act of robbery. They should have felt a similar sense of shame. However, they had become so debased that they bowed before a piece of wood or a stone that had become their idol and acknowledged it as their source of life. But when they found that they were in trouble and that their lifeless gods were unable to help them, they did not hesitate to turn to the God whom they had abandoned and demand that He save them! Without courtesy or respect, they would address God with harsh, emphatic imperatives: "Get up! Save us!" (2:27 JB).

With a touch of sarcasm Jeremiah challenged them to seek help from the many gods they had made. The prophet was not exaggerating when he said, "You have as many gods as you have towns, O Judah" (2:28). It has been estimated that there were more than 250 gods in the neighboring Ugaritic pantheon. In Athens it was said to be easier to find a god than a man (cf. Acts 17:22–23).

4. *Judah's refusal to acknowledge her guilt* (2:29–37)

Using courtroom language again, God asked His people, "Why do you bring charges against me?" (2:29; cf. 2:4–13, where God invited accusation and then accused Judah). They had all rebelled against Him and refused to accept His chastening; they had killed the prophets, and arrogantly proclaimed their freedom to roam (2:29–31). They believed they had been freed from a burdensome bondage to God. But could Israel forget her covenant obligations so easily? Such forgetfulness would seem to be as unnatural and as unlikely as a maiden forgetting to wear her jewels or a bride the sash that marked her as married (2:32; cf. Isa. 3:20). A husband whose bride could never remember to wear her wedding ring would begin to question her love for him.

With concern that is reminiscent of Amos, Jeremiah charged his people with oppression of the poor (2:34). Though their guilt was undeniable, they insisted on their innocence (2:35). Judgment was inevitable because they refused to admit they had sinned. The unrepentant sinner cannot expect God's mercy. Judah's alliances with such foreign powers as Egypt and Assyria rather than God were leading the nation to utter ruin (2:36–37).

C. A Plea to Return to God (3:1–4:4)

1. *Judah as the unfaithful wife* (3:1–5)

God reminded Judah that a husband could not legally take back a faithless wife (3:1; cf. Deut. 24:1–4). The proofs of Judah's infidelity were to be seen everywhere. In their eagerness to embrace every kind of idolatry, the people were like a nomadic bandit awaiting the caravan in order to plunder it (3:2). God had already sent warning of His displeasure by withholding the rain in its season, but the people were unrepentant (3:3; cf. Deut. 11:10–17; Joel 1:17–20; Amos 4:6–12).

Verse 4 is probably a reference to the recent reforms of Josiah. His reign had been a time of national repentance and turning to God; yet it was already forgotten. There was a mistaken attitude that God is so good He will forgive anything!

2. *A comparison of guilt* (3:6–11)

In a message dated in the reign of Josiah (3:6), God made a comparison between "faithless" Israel ("backsliding," KJV; a recurring word in Jeremiah [2:19; 3:14–22; 5:6; 31:22, etc.]) and her "sister" Judah (3:8). Israel had gone after other gods and did not return to the Lord. Therefore God allowed the Assyrians to conquer the nation as a just punishment. Judah saw what had happened to Israel but did not think

God would deal similarly with her. She was pursuing the same course, defiling the land and committing spiritual adultery with stone and wood (3:8–9). Josiah's reforms did not permanently alter the drift into apostasy; so God saw Judah's worship as a "pretense" (3:10). By comparison Israel, for all her wickedness, was pronounced more righteous than Judah (3:11). The reason was that Judah had the benefit of Israel's calamity but ignored the lessons she should have learned (cf. Ezek. 16:51–52).

3. A promise of forgiveness (3:12–18)

God pleaded with Israel that she could still return to Him. The appeal, "Return (the equivalent of "repent" in the Old Testament), faithless Israel" ("backsliding Israel," KJV), occurs frequently in Jeremiah. It represents a play on a single Hebrew word and could be translated, "Turn back, back-turning Israel." However, Jeremiah warned that if she did return, she must confess her iniquity and disobedience (3:13).

Employing a bold figure as the basis of the appeal to return in 3:14, Jeremiah said God was the husband (Hebrew, ba'al). The Hebrew word means "lord" or "master" and is used in other contexts as the name of the Canaanite fertility deity. If Israel, the faithless wife, would return, God would restore the people to Zion and give them rulers ("shepherds," see 2:8) after His own heart (3:15). Then the people will no longer require or even remember the ark of the covenant[6] as a visible symbol of God's presence (3:16), for they will know that He is in their midst. Judah and Israel will be reunited and will return to their own land (3:18; cf. Hos. 1:11; Isa. 11:12–13; Ezek. 37:16–19).

4. A promise of blessing (3:19–4:4)

Again the appeal was made to return in spite of their past treachery. Though daughters did not ordinarily share in the inheritance, God promised they would have a son's share in it (3:19; cf. Num. 36:1–9).

---

[6]The ark, as a symbol of God's presence, was constructed in the desert (Exod. 37:1–9), captured by the Philistines (1 Sam. 4:10–11), returned by them to Beth Shemesh (1 Sam. 6:13–16), later removed to Kiriath Jearim (1 Sam. 7:1), and finally brought to Jerusalem by David (2 Sam. 6:1–15). It was placed in Solomon's temple (1 Kings 8:5–6), redeposited there by Josiah (2 Chron. 35:3), and probably destroyed in 587 or taken to Babylon as a trophy of war. A legend in 2 Maccabees 2:4–7 says that Jeremiah hid the ark in a cave where it will remain undiscovered until God regathers His people. Revelation 11:19 says the "ark of his covenant" is in God's temple in heaven; however, this may be the archetype or heavenly counterpart of the earthly ark.

The people's reply, "Yes, we will come to you" (3:22), may be interpreted as a superficial expression of return (cf. Hos. 6:1). It may express what God wanted them to say, or it may have anticipated a genuine return to God in the future in spite of their present devotion to "shameful gods" (3:24; "the shameful thing," NASB; i.e., Baal).

For Israel to return to God, the people would have to renounce their idols (4:1) and take the solemn oath, "As surely as the LORD lives" (4:2); then He would fulfill the promises made to Abraham (Gen. 12:2–3). This oath, found at least sixty-six times in the Old Testament, was pronounced when a person wanted to emphasize his sincerity or truthfulness. It had the same solemnity as an oath taken today with one's hand on the Bible. If Israel would return to God, other nations also would turn to Him and be blessed (4:2).

Repeating an appeal found in Hosea 10:12, the Lord told Judah, "Break up your unplowed ground" (4:3; "fallow ground," KJV, RSV, NASB). Like hardened soil choked with weeds that must be plowed deep before planting the seed, Judah's repentance needed to be deep and genuine. Judah would also need to do more than continue the outward ritual of circumcision of the flesh in order to be God's people (cf. Gen. 17:11; Rom. 2:28–29). The reference to the circumcision of the heart (Jer. 4:4; cf. Deut. 10:16) indicates that inward commitment had to replace outward ritual or external signs of allegiance to the Lord (cf. Jer. 9:26).

D. Warning of an Invasion from the North (4:5–31)

1. *Announcement of the invasion* (4:5–13)

The warning of coming disaster on Judah is appropriately introduced by an appeal to blow the trumpet (as a signal of approaching danger or as a call to battle) and to seek refuge in the fortified cities (4:5). The evil from the north (cf. 1:13–16) had already set out on its mission of destruction. Though no specific nation is named, the "destroyer of nations" must be Babylon, which is compared to a lion emerging from his lair to seek prey (4:7). When the kings, princes, priests, and prophets see this approaching enemy, they will be appalled (4:9).

Overcome by the vivid description of the impending devastation, Jeremiah protested to God: "How completely you have deceived this people and Jerusalem by saying, 'You will have peace,' when the sword is at our throats" (4:10). For the moment the prophet shared his people's lack of understanding of God's ways. God did promise peace and blessing to His people, but only if they were obedient. Jeremiah should not have been surprised that their faithlessness was bringing the sword rather than peace.

God compared the coming destruction of Jerusalem to a scorching desert wind that withers and destroys the tender plants in its path (4:11). The speaker of "Woe to us! We are ruined!" (4:13) is not identified.

2. An appeal to repent (4:14-18)

It was still not too late for Jerusalem to repent of her evil and be saved. Jeremiah appealed, "O Jerusalem, wash the evil from your heart" (4:14). "Wash" is a word that means "tread" or "subjugate"; here the prophet employed an intensive form of the verb. He meant that the cleansing must be thorough and could be painful. Jerusalem's conduct was bringing bitter punishment on her (4:18).

3. The prophet's anguish (4:19-22)

These verses are frequently referred to as the "cross of Jeremiah." The reader is overwhelmed by the deep emotion of the cry, "My anguish, my anguish" (4:19; literally, "my bowels"; they, not the heart, were considered to be the seat of human emotions). The words are usually understood as the prophet's personal anguish and grief over the imminent invasion. If so, the speaker changes in verse 22, for only God would say, "My people are fools; they do not know me." If, however, God is the speaker throughout these verses, then we are allowed a remarkable glimpse into the anguished heart of God over Judah's coming destruction.

4. A time of chaos and ruin (4:23-31)

The prophet uses language like that found in Genesis 1:2 as he tries to convey the awfulness of the destruction of Judah (4:23). But even while announcing Judah's impending doom, God still held out hope: "I will not destroy it completely" (4:27; "I will not make a full end," KJV; cf. 5:10, 18; 30:11; 46:28). The words suggest the doctrine of a remnant found elsewhere in Jeremiah and other books of the Old Testament (e.g., 6:9; 23:3; 42:19; Amos 5:15; Isa. 11:16; Mic. 2:12; Zeph. 2:9; Hag. 1:12).[7]

---

[7]Read Gerhard F. Hasel, *The Remnant: The History and Theology of the Remnant Idea from Genesis to Isaiah* (Berrien Springs, Mich.: Andrews University Press, 1972) for a study of the remnant. Whatever else the remnant in the Old Testament may imply, it clearly teaches that Israel's hope for the future was based on the grace of God.

The message concludes by addressing Jerusalem as a prostitute dressed in scarlet whose eyes have been shaded with paint (4:30; literally, "you tear with paint," i.e., widen the eyes with cosmetics). She will discover in that terrible time of destruction that her lovers will fail her (4:30; i.e., her allies on whom she had depended). Her cries of anguish will be like those of a woman in childbirth, and her lovers will become her murderers (4:31).

E. The Utter Sinfulness of Judah (5:1–31)

1. *The vain search for one upright person* (5:1–13)

In an effort to demonstrate just how hopeless was the moral condition of Jerusalem, God ordered that a search be made throughout the city for one just person. If such a person could be found, He would pardon the city! (Cf. Gen. 18:22–32 where God agreed to spare Sodom if ten righteous people could be found there.) Since the imperatives in 5:1 are plural, the command was not specifically addressed to Jeremiah but to anyone who would accept the challenge. The searcher would discover that their faces were "harder than stone" and that they would not repent (5:3).

Like Diogenes searching for an honest man, Jeremiah tried to find a just person in Jerusalem. He first went to the poor, thinking that they were surely godly people; but he discovered that they were foolish and did not know the way of the Lord (5:4). He then sought among the leaders, assuming that, with their education and background, they would know the laws of God. However, he had to conclude that all classes, rich and poor, had rebelled and therefore would be punished (5:5–6; cf. Rom. 3:23).

In spite of their material prosperity given by God ("I supplied all their needs," 5:7), they were unfaithful, immoral, without gratitude, and self-sufficient. They were like lusty horses, each neighing after another's wife (5:8). They could expect to be punished for such wickedness (5:9).

The false prophets appear to be the object of God's wrath in verses 10–13. The clause, "He will do nothing" in verse 12 also has been translated, "Not he" (Hebrew; NASB), "It is not he" (KJV), "He is nothing" (JB), and "He does not exist" (NEB). The prophets assured the people that no harm would come to them and that God would do nothing to them. They were like "wind" (5:13; "windbags," *Moffatt*), and God's Word was not in them.

2. *The sending of a faraway nation as punishment* (5:14–31)

To counteract the lying words of the prophets, "the LORD God Almighty" (5:14; "LORD God of Hosts," KJV; a name for God used especially by Isaiah that expresses God's sovereignty over the earthly armies and the heavenly hosts) told Jeremiah that He would "make my words in your mouth a fire." It would consume the people as though they were wood. Again Jeremiah raised the threat of punishment through "an ancient and enduring nation" (5:15; i.e., Babylonia, though not called by name). The Babylonians would destroy the land and the people (5:17) and lead them into captivity (5:19; cf. 5:15–17 with Deut. 28:49–57).

Jeremiah described Israel's rebellion as unnatural and as unexpected as the waves of the ocean trying to pass beyond the boundaries established by the shoreline (5:22). The prophet was saying that the ocean did not transgress the bounds set for it, but Judah did. She had no fear of God, nor did she acknowledge God as the source of the rain in its season (5:24). Wicked men entrapped others like a person who snares birds (5:26). Like a cage filled with small birds to be offered as sacrifices, their houses were filled with wealth gained by deceit (5:27). They were fat (a term of contempt for the rich; e.g., Deut. 32:15; Job 15:27; Ps. 73:7) and sleek (literally, "they shine"), but they had no regard for the poor and orphans (5:28; cf. Exod. 22:22; Deut. 14:29).

Chapter 5 closes by mentioning something horrible and shocking that was happening in the land: "The prophets prophesy lies, the priests rule by their own authority" (i.e., not on the basis of the law), but the people loved it that way (5:31; cf. Amos 4:5). They should have thought beyond the present moment and asked, "But what will you do in the end?" (5:31).

F. Another Warning of Coming Judgment (6:1–30)

1. *A warning to flee the coming siege* (6:1–8)

Jeremiah sounded another warning of coming destruction from the north. Tekoa (twelve miles south of Jerusalem and Amos' hometown) and Beth Hakkerem (location uncertain but probably Tel Ramat Rahel near Jerusalem) would be in the path of the advancing enemy (6:1). The zeal with which the enemy would wreak havoc is noted in the battle cries, "Let us attack at noon! . . . let us attack at night" (6:4–5). Battles were ordinarily begun early in the day and halted at nightfall, but there would be no letup in the siege of Jerusalem. There was no end to her wickedness; it continually poured out like water from a well (6:7).

2. *Punishment for a totally corrupt people* (6:9–15)

Again the Lord made an appeal to search for a faithful remnant so that He might spare them from the coming destruction (cf. 5:1–6). Here the figure used is that of the grape gatherer passing his hand over the branch one more time to see if he has overlooked any grapes (6:9; cf. 49:9). It appeared that no one would listen to Jeremiah's warnings. Their ears were "closed" (6:10; "uncircumcised," KJV). The prophet meant their ears were covered so that they could not hear God's Word (cf. 4:4, "circumcise your hearts").

When he considered the stubborn refusal of the people to heed his warnings, Jeremiah became exasperated. He was ready for the Lord to pour out His wrath on both young and old like scalding water (6:11).

It appeared that everyone in the land had become greedy for personal gain, including prophet and priest. The prophets were giving the people false assurance by telling them that all was well when it was not (6:13–14). Such words were no more helpful than the physician who covers a cancer with a bandage and pronounces it cured. So wicked had the people become that there was no shame. So accustomed were they to wickedness that they no longer knew how to blush (6:15)!

3. *Rejection of the ancient paths* (6:16–21)

The Lord made an appeal to Judah to "ask for the ancient paths, ask where the good way is, and walk in it" (6:16). By so doing they would find inner peace not achieved by their present practices. The words must not be interpreted as an appeal to become an intransigent reactionary who is against all progress and is unwilling to try anything new or different. The "ancient paths" (6:16) were the laws that had been given to their ancestors. Only by keeping the laws of God—walking in the way of righteousness—could they expect to find rest for their souls. Judah, however, refused to walk in the "good way."

Then God reminded them that like watchmen placed on the city wall to warn of approaching danger, so He had sent His prophets to warn the people; but the people refused to listen (6:17; cf. Ezek. 3:17–21; 33:1–19).

Because they had rejected God's laws, their burnt offerings and sacrifices were unacceptable to Him, however costly they might be

(6:20). Jeremiah was not the only prophet to declare, "To obey is better than sacrifice" (1 Sam. 15:22; cf. Amos 5:21–24; Hos. 6:6; Isa. 1:10–20; Mic. 6:6–8). God would put obstacles in the way of His people over which they would stumble and perish (6:21; probably a reference to the enemy from the north).

4. *Terror aroused by the enemy from the north* (6:22–26)

Once again Jeremiah warned of the cruel enemy who would come against Judah from the north (cf. 6:22–24 with 50:41–43, where the enemy from the north is advancing against Babylon). The report of the rapacious horde paralyzed the people with fear but was not sufficient to bring them to repentance. Jeremiah saw "terror on every side" (6:25; a phrase he frequently used; cf. 20:3, 10; 46:5; 49:29). The people should be putting on sackcloth and rolling in ashes, as grief-stricken as a parent who loses an only son, for the destroyer was soon coming (6:26).

5. *Appointment of Jeremiah as assayer* (6:27–30)

God told Jeremiah that He had made him "a tester of metals and my people the ore" (6:27; "an assayer and a tester," NASB; "tower and a fortress," KJV). The NIV and NASB renderings seem to be required by verses 29–30, but if a mixed metaphor may be permitted, "tower and fortress" makes good sense when one remembers the words to Jeremiah in 1:18. Ordinarily the intense heat to which impure metal is subjected is sufficient to separate the dross and leave the pure metal. In Judah's case past warnings and chastisements (6:29, "refining") had been useless; the wicked people were not purged. Therefore, like silver that must be discarded if it cannot be refined, the people of Judah were "rejected silver" (6:30; "reprobate silver," KJV) "because the LORD has rejected them" (6:30).

For Further Study

1. In a Bible dictionary or encyclopedia (see bibliography) read articles on: Baal, Josiah, and prophecy.

2. Make a comparative study of the calls of the prophets found in the Old Testament.

3. What do you understand a "call from God" to mean?

4. Make a study of the Babylonian empire under the rule of Nebuchadnezzar.

Chapter 2

The Temple Sermon and Other Messages of Warning
(Jeremiah 7:1–10:25)

Jeremiah's controversy with his people was based on opposing understandings of God. The people of Judah based their security on God's protective presence guaranteed by the covenant made at Mount Sinai. The temple was a visible symbol of His presence among His people, as the false prophets frequently reassured them. It had become to many a kind of talisman or lucky charm that supposedly warded off evil. Jeremiah understood, however, that Judah could count on God's protection and blessing only if the people obeyed the covenant laws. The conflict between people and prophet was irreconcilable because neither side would adjust its views to accommodate the other.

A. The Temple Sermon and Some Related Warnings (7:1–8:3)

1. *The sermon delivered at the temple* (7:1–15)

Many scholars feel that the temple sermon recorded in 7:1–15 is the same as the sermon of chapter 26. If so, this is the first of Jeremiah's messages that can be dated with some certainty, for 26:1 says it was "early in the reign of Jehoiakim," perhaps 608 B.C. If the two chapters describe the same event, chapter 7 gives its major emphasis to the message that was preached, whereas chapter 26 gives more attention to reactions to the message.

The year 608 B.C. was one of crisis. Nineveh had fallen; Babylon was maneuvering her military machine for a showdown with Egypt; Judah had a new, untested king. In such uncertain times the people turned for reassurance to the temple as a visible symbol of stability and of God's protecting presence. They remembered when Jerusalem had been delivered from the Assyrians, and they believed it would happen again (2 Kings 18:17–19:37). Jeremiah took his life in his hands by attacking the temple. It was considered blasphemous to announce that God's presence in the temple would not protect the people.

When the Lord instructed Jeremiah to "stand at the gate of the LORD's house and there proclaim" (7:2), it may have been during one of the religious festivals when a great crowd would have been there. The gate where he stood probably separated the outer from the inner court.

Once again Jeremiah couched his message in the language of the courtroom. He said prophets were deceiving the people to trust in the temple (7:4). They believed that divine election entitled them to all the covenant privileges but failed to understand that God expected a response of obedience. In verses 5–7 Jeremiah reviewed the spirit of the Deuteronomic law (i.e., "obey and you will be blessed"; cf. Deut. 7:12–15; 28:1–2). These verses contain one of the finest Old Testament summaries of true religion (cf. Ezek. 18:5–9). Protection was assured only by their moral uprightness and faithfulness to God.

Then in 7:8–11 the prophet made his indictment. The people had broken the laws of God (at least six of the Ten Commandments are mentioned) and had given their allegiance to other gods. Jeremiah said they had made the temple a "den of robbers" (7:11; cf. Matt. 21:13; Mark 11:17). However, in spite of all their sins, they still felt secure.

In 7:12–15 the judicial sentence was pronounced. Jerusalem was warned to remember the fate of Shiloh, which once had been the location of the sanctuary (Josh. 18:1; 1 Sam. 1:3).[1] The fact that the tabernacle had been located there did not protect it from destruction. The ark was taken captive by the Philistines (1 Sam. 4), and Shiloh never regained its prominence as a religious center. Judah would be cast out of God's sight, even as Ephraim (i.e., Israel) had been (7:15).

2. No intercession allowed (7:16–20)

As if anticipating a plea from Jeremiah on behalf of Judah, the Lord forbade him to intercede on her behalf (7:16; cf. 11:14; 14:11). The prophet only needed to see what the people were doing to see how useless intercession would be. The entire family was involved in wor-

---

[1]At one time some scholars believed Jeremiah was referring to a destruction of Shiloh by the Philistines ca. 1050 B.C. Others believed he was referring to an eighth-century destruction by the Assyrians. Recent interpretation of the archaeological evidence, however, does not support a destruction of Shiloh until ca. 600 B.C. Jeremiah was probably not referring to the destruction of the city but to the destruction and abandonment of its sanctuary.

shiping the "Queen of Heaven" (7:18). Mentioned only here and in 44:17–25, she may have been the equivalent of the Assyrian-Babylonian Ishtar or the Canaanite Astarte (Ashtoreth), both fertility goddesses. The Queen of Heaven is also mentioned in an Egyptian inscription. God said the people of Judah gave their offerings to other deities in order "to provoke me to anger" (7:18). However, they were only hurting themselves because God's wrath was going to be poured out on them like fire that could not be quenched (7:19–20).

3. *Obedience is better than sacrifice* (7:21–28)

At first glance verse 22 seems to say that God gave no regulations concerning burnt offerings and sacrifice at the time of the Exodus (cf. Amos 5:25). However, such an interpretation would deny that there were sacrifices during the desert period as described in Exodus, Leviticus, and Numbers. God was really saying that sacrifice was not the most important condition for maintaining the covenant relationship with Him. Sacrifice was an expression of obedience, but its value was nullified by acts of disobedience. For centuries, even from the time they left Egypt, the Israelites refused to listen to "my servants the prophets" (7:25), who warned them that they were not obeying God.

4. *Judgment on human sacrifice* (7:29–8:3)

This section begins with a command to cut off the hair as an act of mourning (7:29; cf. Job 1:20; Mic. 1:16; Ezek. 19:1), for God had rejected His people because of their abominable practices. The command to cut the hair perhaps alludes to the Nazirite vow (Num. 6:5) that required the hair to remain uncut, thus symbolizing one's dedication to God. Here the prophet's command to cut the hair would symbolize that the Nazirite vow of loyalty had been broken.

The people defiled the temple by placing idols in it (7:30; cf. Ezek. 8). They also offered their own children as human sacrifices at Topheth ("place of fire"), south of Jerusalem in the Valley of Ben Hinnom (7:31; Gehenna in the New Testament).[2] This was done even though human sacrifice was specifically forbidden by Mosaic law (Lev. 18:21; 20:2–5).

---

[2]The belief that the Valley of Hinnom was a public garbage heap and incinerator into which unclean corpses were cast and therefore the origin of the transfer of the name to Gehenna as a place of fiery punishment for the wicked has been disproved by archaeological studies. Gehenna more likely became associated with the underworld because of the altars erected there to underworld deities such as Molech, to whom the Israelites offered their children as sacrifices.

The time would come when the valley would be called the Valley of Slaughter because of the great number of corpses that would be cast there during the destruction of Jerusalem (7:32–33). The slaughterers of their own children would in turn be slaughtered by the Babylonians.

The enemy would disinter the bones of kings, princes, priests, prophets, and ordinary citizens (8:1). They would scatter them on the ground as an act of insult and contempt. Desecration of graves or lack of proper burial was abhorrent to the Hebrews and other ancient peoples because of the popular belief that immortality was dependent on proper burial. Ironically, the bones would be spread out in view of the sun, the moon, and stars that had been objects of worship by the people of Judah. These false deities would give no protection from the enemy. The people's remains would be scattered like dung on the ground (8:2).

B. Punishment of a Backsliding People (8:4–9:26)

1. *The unnaturalness of Judah's backsliding* (8:4–7)

By means of a series of questions and illustrations, Jeremiah showed that Judah's backsliding was unnatural and without precedent. He pointed out that the person who falls down will get up, and the person who turns away will turn back (i.e., repent; 8:4). However, Jerusalem had turned away, and no one repented of his wickedness (8:5–6; the same verb is used three different ways in 8:5; RSV: "turned away," "backsliding," "return"). The people had deliberately sinned, acting "like a horse charging into battle" (8:6).

Jeremiah observed that the birds in the sky by instinct know when to migrate from one place to another. It should have been just as natural for God's people, endowed with reason, to know what He required of them, but they did not (8:7).

2. *A false claim of wisdom* (8:8–12)

The people of Judah claimed to be wise, for they had the law of the Lord. But their scribes, those who knew the law and perhaps wrote expositions on it, handled it falsely (8:8). Their wise men would be put to shame because they had rejected the Lord's word (8:9). Because of their faithlessness, all would be taken from them, including their wives and fields, and be given to others (8:10).

Jeremiah compared the religious leaders to physicians who gave superficial treatment, for the leaders were assuring Judah that all was well when it was not (8:11; cf. 6:14). They had no shame for what they had done (8:12; cf. 6:15).

3. *The people's despair over the coming invasion* (8:13–17)

Jeremiah said Judah was going to be removed like the unfruitful vine or fig tree that is no longer useful (8:13; cf. Mark 11:12–14; John 15:2). His words describe total apostasy.

Verse 14 gives one of the rare responses to Jeremiah's messages by the people. If what he said was true and they were under God's judgment, they insisted that they should take refuge in the fortified cities and there await their end (8:14). They admitted they had sinned, but there was no expression of repentance. To underscore the certainty of their doom, God added that He was sending "snakes" (i.e., Babylon) against them that would not be charmed into harmlessness (8:17; snake charming is still practiced in the East). Jeremiah may have been alluding to the experience in the desert when God provided an antidote for the poisonous bites of snakes He had sent among the complaining Israelites (Num. 21:6–9). The difference was that the snakes about to be sent could not be placated.

4. *Grief for the stricken people* (8:18–9:9)

These verses are probably responsible for gaining for Jeremiah the reputation of the "weeping prophet." However, if one understands that God is the speaker instead of Jeremiah, then we have one of the most remarkable glimpses of God's compassionate nature in the Bible outside the Cross itself.

In support of God as the speaker, He is clearly speaking in 8:19; 9:3, 6, 9. Further support is the frequent mention of "my people," for this is covenant language used by a sovereign for his vassals (cf. 30:22; Exod. 3:7; 5:1). If God is the speaker in 8:21, the pathos of the brokenness of God over the sins of His people is matched only by such passages as Luke 13:34; 23:28; John 11:35. Ezekiel 6:9 literally describes God as "broken by their adulterous hearts."

Not even the medicinal balm for which Gilead, a region east of the Jordan, was famous could heal the spiritual sickness of Judah (8:22). The thought of the coming slaughter of "my people" was sufficient to cause the tears to flow without ceasing (9:1; cf. Elisha, who wept by anticipation when he considered the evil that Hazael was going to bring to Israel, 2 Kings 8:11–12). For a moment there was a deep desire to get away from "my people," for they were all wicked (9:2). They lied, they did not know the Lord, and they plotted against one another. They deceived (9:4; literally, "supplanted," an unmistakable pun on Jacob's name, for "Jacob" comes from this same word; they were all "Jacobs"). They slandered and did not speak an occasional untruth but trained themselves to lie (9:5). Their tongues were deadly arrows; they could speak reassuring words to a neighbor at the same time that they were plotting his ruin (9:8). Was not God justified in punishing such a people (9:9)?

5. *Lament over the destruction of Judah* (9:10–22)

The question of identity of the speaker continues in the 'Hebrew of these verses. The omission of quotation marks in verse 10 means the NIV translators felt Jeremiah was weeping and wailing in that verse, but it could have been God (NASB, RSV). Verse 11 suggests that God is the speaker in both verses (NASB, RSV). Translations that make Jeremiah the speaker in verse 10 and God the speaker in verse 11 arbitrarily place quotation marks around 9:11 (NIV).

Was there anyone wise enough in the land to understand why Judah was being devastated (9:12)? The Lord's answer was that they had forsaken His law and had not obeyed His voice (9:13). They were following the "stubbornness of their hearts" (9:14) and worshiping Baal. Therefore, He would feed them with "bitter food and . . . poisoned water" (9:15; "wormwood and . . . water of gall," KJV) and scatter them among the nations (9:16). In the KJV "wormwood" refers to a plant with a bitter taste; "gall" was a poisonous herb. Thus the figure speaks of a doomed people.

A call was extended for the professional mourners to come and begin their mournful wailing (9:17–18). Jeremiah personified death as a thief creeping into the windows of the palaces and homes to cut off the people in the prime of life (9:21). He warned that there would be no one to bury the dead. Their bodies would lie like dung on the ground and like grain left by the reaper (9:22).

6. *The only basis for boasting* (9:23–24)

People boasted of their wisdom, power, and riches—the usual things about which people brag. However, the Lord said the only thing a person should boast about is that "he understands and knows me" (9:24; cf. 1 Cor. 1:31; 2 Cor. 10:17; Gal. 6:14).

7. *Punishment of the uncircumcised* (9:25–26)

Jeremiah earlier had stressed the need for a circumcised heart (4:4). Now God warned that the time was coming when those circumcised in the flesh but not in the heart would be punished (9:25–26; cf. Gal. 5:6; 6:15). It is significant that Judah was not singled out for favor. She is listed in the midst of Egypt, Edom, Ammon, and Moab (9:26), all of whom also practiced circumcision.

The expression "in distant places" (9:26) is variously translated to produce the idea of universal judgment (cf. "in the utmost corners," KJV; "haunt the fringes of the desert," NEB).

However, other translations take the Hebrew phrase to mean some kind of religious rite: "who clip the hair on their temples" (NASB); "that cut the corners of their hair" (RSV); "shave their temples" (NAB); "Crop-Heads" (JB). If these translations are correct, they refer to a pagan practice of offering one's hair as a sacrifice to a deity, a practice that was forbidden in Israel (Lev. 19:27; 21:5; cf. Jer. 25:23; 49:32). The Hebrew literally says, "those trimmed/cut of the edge/side," so it could be interpreted either to mean universal judgment or a religious rite. The important lesson to observe is that Judah was no different from her neighbors. Though circumcised, she was uncircumcised in heart.

C. The Foolishness of Idolatry (10:1–25)

No sin is condemned more severely or more frequently in the Old Testament than idolatry, the worship of a deity carved from wood, stone, or some other material. It was a sin that attracted Israel early (Exod. 32; Num. 25:1–3) despite a specific prohibition against idols (Exod. 20:4–6). The prophets compared idolatry to harlotry (Hos. 5:3–4), but no one ridiculed and denounced idolatry with greater sarcasm than Jeremiah and Isaiah (cf. Isa. 40:18–20; 41:5–7, 21–24, 28–29; 44:9–20; 45:16, 20; 46:1–7).

1. *Contrast between God and idols* (10:1–16)

Belief that gods could reside in stone or wood representations was widely held in the ancient world. However, Israel was warned, "Do not learn the ways of the nations" (10:2). It was also believed that these gods could be controlled to work on behalf of the worshiper if he performed certain rituals or repeated prescribed incantations. Jeremiah ridiculed these beliefs; he insisted that idols were "worthless" (10:3; "delusion," NASB; cf. Rom. 1:21–23). After all, these idols were nothing but a tree cut from the forest, shaped by craftsmen, and decorated with silver from Tarshish (probably Tartessus in Spain) and gold from Uphaz (location unknown). They were then fastened securely so they would not topple over (10:4).

Jeremiah heaped further scorn on the idols by comparing them to a "scarecrow in a melon patch" (10:5; "upright as the palm tree," KJV). They could not speak or walk; therefore, there was no need to fear them. They could not harm or help anyone; they were nongods.

By striking contrast Jeremiah then insisted, "No one is like you, O LORD" (10:6). He further affirmed that God was the "King of the nations" (10:7), the true and "living God," and "the eternal King" (10:10). No nation could stand before the wrath of God, and the nongods would "perish from the earth and from under the heavens" (10:11; this verse is in Aramaic; other Old Testament sections preserved in Aramaic rather than Hebrew are Dan. 2:4b–7:28; Ezra 4:8–6:18; 7:12–26). These are words of a monotheistic faith that eventually characterized the Hebrew people.

After ridiculing the helplessness of the idols, Jeremiah went on to contrast the power of the living God (10:12–16; cf. 51:15–19). He acknowledged Him as the Creator of heaven and earth and the One who controls the rain and wind. He called Him the "Portion of Jacob" (10:16; "Jacob's Creator," NEB; cf. Deut. 32:9). God is not like the worthless idols. He is the "Maker of all things, including Israel, the tribe of his inheritance" (10:16).

2. The coming destruction and scattering of the flock (10:17–25)

Jeremiah foresaw the impending invasion and siege and appealed to the people of Jerusalem to gather their belongings and prepare for flight (10:17–18). The speaker in verses 19–22 appears to be the land itself as it surveys its ruin and destruction. The shepherds (rulers) were responsible for the scattering of the flock (the people) because they were stupid and had not sought the Lord (10:21).

The chapter concludes with an acknowledgment that man does not have the ability to direct his own steps (10:23; cf. Prov. 3:5–6; Ps. 37:23). Jeremiah was willing to accept the Lord's chastening but asked that it not be done in anger, lest he be destroyed (10:24). Then he asked the Lord to pour out His wrath on those people who had harmed Israel (10:25; cf. 18:23; Ps. 79:6–7). His very human response could be paraphrased, "Deal gently with me, O LORD, but deal harshly with my enemies!" This and other prayers throughout the book have earned Jeremiah the reputation of "the father of true prayer."

For Further Study

1. In a Bible dictionary or encyclopedia (see bibliography) read articles on: Queen of Heaven, burial, Gehenna, and balm.

2. What does the temple sermon teach about putting one's trust in organized religion?

3. Why is obedience more important to God than sacrifices and offerings?

4. Why was human sacrifice so widespread in the ancient world and so abhorrent to God?

5. How is idolatry practiced today?

Chapter 3

Times of Crisis in Jeremiah's Life
(Jeremiah 11:1–15:21)

Chapters 11–20 contain the most personal glimpses into the soul of a prophet found in the Bible. The so-called "confessions" of Jeremiah (also called soliloquies, monologues, dialogues, prayers, laments, and intimate papers) are found in 11:18–23; 12:1–6; 15:10–21; 17:12–18; 18:18–23; 20:7–18. They reveal with remarkable candor the inner struggles and humanity of a prophet during times of personal crisis.

We are grateful that Jeremiah had the courage to share these most intimate thoughts. He could have suppressed them and perhaps preserved a more heroic image. The "confessions" are largely responsible for the ready identification that most people have with Jeremiah among the prophets. The struggle between freedom to choose one's own way and the compulsion to obey God is at the heart of the "confessions." This same tension is also seen in Job, Habakkuk, Jonah, Elijah, and with our Lord in Gethsemane.

A. Jeremiah and the Covenant (11:1–17)

1. *Jeremiah's proclamation of the covenant* (11:1–8)

A covenant is an agreement between two or more parties that involves mutual obligations. Judah's accountability to God was based on the covenant made with Israel at Sinai, though some scholars interpret "this covenant" (11:2) as a reference only to the Book of Deuteronomy.

Judah had forgotten the covenant as well as the punishment inflicted on her ancestors who also stubbornly disobeyed God. God found it necessary to remind Judah of her covenant obligations. He warned of the curse on those who would not heed the covenant (11:3; cf. Deut. 11:28; 27:15–26). The forefathers had been delivered from slavery in

Egypt, a bondage Jeremiah called "the iron-smelting furnace" (11:4; a metaphor for harsh affliction; cf. Deut. 4:20; 1 Kings 8:51). After leaving Egypt and arriving at Mount Sinai, the people received the Mosaic law, which was their national constitution. Afterward, God brought them into a land flowing with milk and honey. Jeremiah affirmed that all God said was true by responding, "Amen" (11:5; from a word meaning "be secure," "to endure," or "to support"; cf. Deut. 27:26). But in spite of all God had done for them, the people chose to walk in "the stubbornness of their evil hearts" (11:8).

2. Punishment for breaking the covenant (11:9–13)

Because the present generation "returned to the sins of their forefathers" (11:10), God was going to bring disaster on them (11:11). They would cry to their gods who were as numerous as their cities, but their gods could not save them (11:12–13; cf. 2:28).

3. Jeremiah forbidden to intercede (11:14–17)

Again God cautioned Jeremiah not to pray for the people, for it would do no good (11:14; cf. 7:16). They had no right to be in His temple because of their evil deeds (11:15). God compared them to a luxuriant olive tree whose worthless branches are set on fire (11:16). Judgment was coming because they had provoked God by offering sacrifices to Baal (11:17).

B. A Plot Against Jeremiah's Life (11:18–12:6)

1. Reaction of the men of Anathoth to Jeremiah (11:18–23)

Jeremiah's preaching usually achieved no results except violence directed against himself. God revealed to him a plot against his life concocted by men of his own hometown, Anathoth. No specific reason is given for their desire to kill him, but it must have grown out of their dislike for his prophecies. Jeremiah had been unaware of what was happening ("like a gentle lamb led to the slaughter," 11:19). But when he learned of the plot, his reaction was very human. He asked that God bring vengeance on his enemies (11:20). In every one of Jeremiah's "confessions" found in chapters 11–20, there is a similar appeal for vengeance. We would have preferred to hear, "Father, forgive them, for they do not know what they are doing" (Luke 23:34); but Jeremiah was human, not divine.

The Lord responded to the prophet's call for vengeance by assuring him that the conspirators would be punished. "The year of their punishment" (11:23) probably anticipates the destruction of Jerusalem in 587 B.C.

2. Jeremiah questions the prosperity of the wicked (12:1-6)

Scholars are divided as to whether 12:1-6 is a continuation of the previous "confession" or one that was occasioned by another situation. Some believe that more logically 11:18-23 should follow 12:1-6. Jeremiah raised the age-old question, "Why does the way of the wicked prosper?" (12:1; cf. Job 21:7; Hab. 1:2-4; Mal. 2:17; 3:14-15; Pss. 37; 49; 73). However, he was careful not to question God's righteousness (12:1). The "wicked" for Jeremiah may have been those men of Anathoth who plotted against him. God appeared to be blessing them ("they . . . bear fruit"), but their loyalty to Him was superficial ("You are . . . far from their hearts," 12:2).

His cry for vengeance was stronger than in 11:20. Now he says, "Drag them off (a word that can be used of ripping up tent cords; cf. Isa. 33:20) like sheep to be butchered!" (12:3). They taunted him in reply, "He will not see what happens to us" (12:4). If they meant God will not see, they were accusing Him of indifference or inability to know about their evil deeds. If they meant Jeremiah, they were threatening that he would not outlive them.

God's answer to Jeremiah contained a gentle rebuke (12:5). If a footrace with men tired him, how could he compete in a race with horses? If he could not stand up on level ground, what would happen to him in the "thickets" ("swelling," KJV) of the Jordan? God was warning that the difficulties Jeremiah had experienced were mild in comparison to what lay ahead. He seemed to be saying, "Cheer up, Jeremiah, the worst is yet to come!" A person who cannot cope with his own problems is hardly suitable to help others with theirs.

The Lord added a further caution to Jeremiah not to be deceived by friendly words of his own family (12:6). No direct answer to Jeremiah's question concerning the prosperity of the wicked is given here or elsewhere in the Bible.

C. God's People and Their Neighbors (12:7-17)

1. God's lament for His devastated people (12:7-13)

God found it necessary to give His people into the hands of the enemy (12:7). His inheritance had turned on Him like a savage lion

(12:8) and was like a conspicuous "speckled bird of prey" (12:9); "hyena's lair," NEB). He invited the wild beasts to devour Judah. He accused the shepherds (leaders) of ruining His vineyard and turning the land into a desolate wasteland (12:10). The desolation was at hand because no one cared (12:11). The harvest of Judah's wickedness was about to come on its inhabitants, and they would bear their shame (12:13, cf. Hos. 8:7; Gal. 6:7).

2. *Judgment and mercy on neighboring peoples* (12:14–17)

The dual theme of God's judgment and His love for His people occurs frequently in the Bible. A threat mingled with a note of compassion for Israel's enemies is less frequent. Jeremiah announced that God was going to uproot Judah's wicked neighbors, but He would later return them to their own lands (12:14–15). He promised to bless those nations who would accept Him (12:16). Those who refused to listen would be destroyed (12:17). The Abrahamic promises of Genesis 12:1–3 are implied here. The passage teaches the universal sovereignty of God over all peoples.

D. Warnings and Laments (13:1–27)

1. *Warning of the ruined linen garment* (13:1–11)

Revelation came to the prophets in many ways—the spoken word, visions, dreams, the Urim and Thummim, etc. One of the most effective modes of revelation was the symbolic act, sometimes called an enacted parable. In this type of revelation the Lord would instruct the prophet to perform a certain act, usually in the presence of an audience. It was a visual aid designed to suggest the larger message that would later be explained to the spectators. However, it was more than a visual aid, for like a word spoken by God, it was believed that the symbolic act actually set in motion the event itself. It was an effective attention getter for a people who were usually indifferent to the prophets' messages.

Jeremiah performed more symbolic acts than any other prophet. Chapter 13 contains the first of them (unless 5:1–6 is also included).[1] God instructed the prophet to purchase a "linen belt" (13:1), which was a kind of undergarment. He was to put it on without first washing it to

[1]Other symbolic acts of Jeremiah are found in 16:1–4; 16:5–13; 18:1–12; 19:1–15; 25:15–29; 27–28; 32:1–15; 35:1–19; 51:59–64.

soften it for greater comfort. Then he was instructed to take it to "Perath" and bury it. The Hebrew word for "Perath" has been a problem for commentators here; it is the usual Hebrew word for "Euphrates." Because of the great distance required by such a journey (it involved traveling at least 350 miles each way) some commentaries suggest he took the garment to the village of Parah (Josh. 18:23), a few miles from Anathoth, where there was an abundant supply of water, or to Perath (NIV, NEB), or to the Parath River (NAB), all being similar in Hebrew to "Euphrates." The purpose would be served by any of these translations; but there is no valid reason for denying the longer journey, especially as it would have been more impressive to the people. Later Jeremiah was told to go and uncover the garment. He, of course, found it rotted and totally useless.

The message of the symbolic act was clear. The garment represented Judah. By wearing it, Jeremiah demonstrated God's closeness to Judah (13:11). The rotted garment represented a sinful people who were no longer of any use to God. They had clung to Baal rather than to God.

2. Warning of the proverb about wine jars (13:12–14)

Prophets frequently made use of popular proverbs in their messages (cf. 17:11; Ezek. 18:2). Jeremiah quoted a well-known proverb, "Every wineskin should be filled with wine" (13:12; "Every jug is to be filled with wine," NASB; in the context an earthen jar is intended). It was such a truism that Jeremiah could expect hecklers to respond, "Don't we know that?" (13:12; "Do you think we do not know that?" JB). Jeremiah was instructed to reply that the jar of the proverb represented all the people of Judah, including their rulers. They would be filled with wine to the point of drunkenness, perhaps an allusion to drinking the cup of wrath (cf. 25:15–29) or to their helplessness at the time of destruction. While they were in such a condition, God would come and destroy them without pity (13:14).

3. A warning against pride (13:15–19)

Jeremiah appealed to the people to abandon their pride and give glory (i.e., honor) to God (13:16; cf. Josh. 7:19, where it means "confess your sin"). Jeremiah wept for the king and his mother and others of Judah who had been taken into exile (13:17–18). The reference is to the captivity of Jehoiachin in 597 at the age of eighteen after a reign of only three months (cf. 2 Kings 24:8–15).

4. *The inevitability of punishment* (13:20–27)

Once again Jeremiah warned that an enemy from the north was coming (13:20). The people would experience pain like that of a mother in childbirth when their former allies and friends came as their conquerors (13:21). Jeremiah anticipated that they would ask why the calamity had happened to them. His answer would be, "It is because of your many sins" (13:22). They would be treated as harshly as a captive led away to slavery or a harlot publicly shamed by exposure. It was as hopeless for Judah to change her ways as for the Ethiopian (literally, "Cushite") to change the color of his skin or for a leopard to change its spots (13:23).

Because their sin habit was so deeply ingrained, God was going to scatter them like straw in the wind (13:24). He would strip them bare like the harlot who was publicly humiliated by exposure (13:26; cf. Hos. 2:3).

Though the situation seemed hopeless, Jeremiah closed his message by holding out a word of hope: "How long will you be unclean?" (13:27). Judah did not need to remain unclean. The mingled messages of judgment and hope were characteristic of the prophets.

E. Catastrophes That Cannot Be Avoided (14:1–15:9)

1. *Drought* (14:1–6)

If the rains did not fall in their season in the Near East, the resulting "drought" (14:1; literally "droughts"; "dearth," KJV) could be catastrophic. The crops would not grow, and famine was inevitable. Cisterns would dry up, and the people would search in vain for water to drink.

Jeremiah described in these verses the effects of a severe drought that was afflicting the land and used the occasion to warn Judah (cf. 3:3; 12:4; 23:10). Elsewhere we are told that God withheld the rain as a warning of His displeasure and of greater judgment (Deut. 28:12, 23–24; Amos 4:7–8).

"Servants" (literally, "little ones," KJV, but not the usual word for servant) sent by their masters to seek water returned with their jars empty and their heads covered as a gesture of grief and confusion (14:3; cf. 2 Sam. 15:30; 19:4). Farmers looked at the cracked ground and covered their heads in grief also (14:4). Animals gave birth to their young but quickly abandoned them, for there was no grass to be found for food (14:5). Wild donkeys stood on the hillsides panting for air in the searing heat and looked in vain for food (14:6).

2. *A plea for mercy* (14:7–9)

The speaker in these verses may have been the people of Judah who were constantly disobedient but who felt they could call on God in time of trouble (cf. 7:9–10). However, the speaker was more likely Jeremiah, voicing a confession on behalf of his people (cf. 14:11). The plea was for God to act for "the sake of your name" (14:7). The phrase, found frequently (e.g., Ps. 31:3; Isa. 66:5; Ezek. 20:9), was an appeal to God to maintain the honor of His reputation by acting with mercy.

It was believed in the ancient world that a name revealed something about a person's nature. God's name was His essential nature, His very character. A study of the various names for God in the Old Testament reveal many of His attributes (e.g., power, self-existence). Jeremiah acknowledged that God was the "Hope of Israel, its Savior" (14:8; cf. 17:13; Acts 28:20; Col. 1:27). He appealed to God not to be indifferent, as though He were a stranger in the land or a traveler pitching his tent for a night before passing on (14:8).

The plea closed with a bold, almost presumptuous, question about God's ability to save His people. Was He "taken by surprise" (14:9; "astonied," KJV; "asleep," LXX; the word means to be surprised or bewildered)? Was He like a "warrior" (14:9; "mighty man," RSV) who failed in time of danger when most needed? Since He dwelt in their midst and they were called by His name (i.e., they belonged to Him through a covenant relationship), the appeal implied that God must act to preserve His reputation among the heathen.

3. *The Lord's reply (14:10–12)*

The reply to Jeremiah's plea makes it clear that the petitioner was Jeremiah. God rejected the appeal for mercy by reminding Jeremiah that the people loved to wander, and so it was time to call them to judgment (14:10; cf. Hos. 8:13). As on other occasions (e.g., 7:16; 11:14), God told the prophet not to pray for the people (14:11). He would no longer hear their cries or accept their offerings (14:12). He had determined to destroy them. The rejection of Jeremiah's prayers must not be understood as indifference or lack of compassion. It was based on the reality of the situation. Judah's heart was so hardened that nothing would change her; she had sealed her own doom.

4. *Judgment on the false prophets* (14:13-16)

In a bold rejoinder to God's rejection of his pleas for Judah, Jeremiah pointed out that the people were being led astray by false prophets. These men were giving assurance that neither foe nor famine would overtake them (14:13). The Lord agreed with Jeremiah that the prophets had misled the people. Their visions were false; their divinations were useless; their prophecies came from the "delusions of their own minds" (Hebrew, "heart," 14:14) and they would perish (14:15). However, God did not excuse the people because they listened to the false prophets. They would experience famine and the sword, with no one to bury them. God would pour out on them "the calamity they deserve" (14:16; "their wickedness on them," KJV, NASB, RSV).

5. *The prophet's lament* (14:17-18)

The speaker of this lament is generally considered to be the weeping prophet, Jeremiah. However, the same question of interpretation must be raised here that was considered with 8:18-9:9. Is this another account of God weeping for "my people" (14:17)? The designation of Judah as the "virgin daughter" does not conflict with comparisons elsewhere of her to a harlot (cf. Amos 5:2; Jer. 46:11; Isa. 47:1). It could be understood as an idealistic description of what Judah should be, or it may mean that she had been protected from harm up to that time.

Judah's devastation was compared to a grievous wound. Those slain by the sword and famine would be found everywhere. The prophets and priests were going "to a land they know not," i.e., into exile (14:18; the verb may mean, however, that they were wandering about in their own land not knowing what to do; cf. "ply their trade through the land," RSV; "go begging round the land," NEB).

6. *Another appeal to God* (14:19-22)

Though the Lord had already told Jeremiah not to pray for Judah (14:11), the prophet could not restrain himself. He wanted to know if God had completely rejected Judah. Did He despise her? Had He so afflicted her that there was no possibility for healing (14:19)? Jeremiah acknowledged Judah's wickedness (14:20), but unfortunately Judah did not. Once again he pleaded with God to act in such a way that His reputation would be preserved (14:21; cf. 14:9; Exod. 32:11-14; Num. 14:13-19). He appealed to the Lord not to disgrace the throne of His glory (i.e., Jerusalem; cf. 3:17), nor to break His covenant (14:21). The basis for Jeremiah's appeal was threefold: God's name (His reputation), His city (Jerusalem), and His covenant.

One of the Lord's principal grievances against His people was that they gave credit to Baal (a storm god) for the rain in its seasons and for the soil's fertility, rather than acknowledging that these things came from God (see Hos. 2:5, 8). Jeremiah confessed what God wanted all Judah to admit—that only the Lord their God could provide the rain. Then Jeremiah concluded, "Our hope is in you" (14:22). This was what God wanted all Judah to acknowledge, but unfortunately Jeremiah was speaking only for himself.

7. The Lord's reply (15:1-4)

The fervency of Jeremiah's intercession on behalf of his people is matched in the Old Testament only by Moses and Samuel, who in their times had frequently moved God by their appeals (cf. Exod. 32:11-14, 30; Num. 14:13-19; 1 Sam. 7:8; 12:19-23). God's reply to Jeremiah's pleas, however, was unyielding. God said that even if Moses and Samuel stood before Him and pleaded for Judah, it would do no good (15:1).

If the people came to Jeremiah asking, "Where shall we go?" God advised him to tell them that they were destined to go to death, sword, starvation, and captivity (15:2). God seemed to be saying, "I don't care any longer what happens to Judah. I will no longer help her." He warned that He was sending the sword to kill and the dogs to drag away and the birds and the wild beasts to devour and destroy (15:3).

God threatened to make Judah abhorrent in all the earth because of what Manasseh had done while he was Judah's king (15:4). Manasseh had the longest reign of any king of Judah and was probably the most wicked. He encouraged Baal worship, built altars for astral deities in the temple, offered his own son as a human sacrifice, and practiced witchcraft and divination (2 Kings 21:1-18).

Judgment was coming on the present generation of Judah, but not because of what Manasseh did in his time. However, because he had encouraged idolatrous practices, his influence extended to the present generation. It was still doing the same things. This passage must be interpreted in the light of other statements of Jeremiah (31:29-30; cf. Ezek. 18:2-4). God does not punish one generation for the sins of a previous generation; each one is punished for its own sins.

8. *No more pity* (15:5–9)

God warned that there would be no one to mourn or pity Jerusalem or even ask about her welfare (15:5). She had forgotten God and was getting progressively worse. He said, "You keep on backsliding" (15:6). He would no longer relent; He was going to destroy Jerusalem. He planned to winnow her with a winnowing fork, a reference to the common practice of farmers pitching grain into the air with a fork (15:7). The wind blows away the chaff as the grain falls to the ground. The metaphor describes the separation of the good from the wicked (cf. Luke 3:17).

God announced that He would bring bereavement and destruction and make their widows more numerous than the sand of the seas. Mothers of choice young men would not escape. Destruction was coming suddenly and swiftly (15:7–8). The prophet referred to the mother of "seven" (15:9), using the number of perfection in the sense of representing complete happiness that has turned to total despair. As a result she would breathe her last. The sons who survived the initial slaughter would become prisoners of the enemy and be killed. These ominous words should have terrified the inhabitants of Jerusalem, but no one paid any attention.

F. Jeremiah's Lament and God's Rebuke (15:10–21)

In these verses we have the third of Jeremiah's confessions (cf. 11:18–23; 12:1–6), and the first in which God severely rebuked Jeremiah for his complaints.

Regretting that he had been born (cf. 20:14–18; Job 3), Jeremiah lamented the fact that his faithful ministry had brought him nothing but unpopularity and persecution. Though he had neither lent nor borrowed money, everyone was cursing him (15:10; cf. Deut. 23:19–20). He reminded the Lord that He had promised good things to him and that even his enemies would plead with him in the time of disaster (15:11), but none of this was happening.

The meaning of 15:12–13 is uncertain. If Jeremiah was the speaker, he was saying that the task before him was as impossible as smashing iron or bronze (incorrectly "steel," KJV). The words may mean that it was impossible to overcome the enemy from the north. "Iron from the north" (15:12) may refer to iron that was unusually hard and from a geographical region to the north as a figure for the difficulty of Jeremiah's task. Whatever the interpretation, Jeremiah was clearly discouraged. The land was going to be despoiled of its wealth because of God's wrath and its people taken captive (15:13–14; cf. 17:3–4), but no one would listen to Jeremiah's warnings.

In a mood of self-pity, Jeremiah defended his zeal for the Lord's cause. He pleaded for vengeance on his persecutors on the basis of the reproach he had suffered for the Lord's sake (15:15). He remembered his initial call, his wholehearted acceptance of God's words that became a joy and a delight to him (15:16; cf. Ezek. 2:8–3:3; Rev. 10:9–10).

He reminded the Lord that he had not joined with the merrymakers. In fact, because God's hand was on him, he was all alone (15:17; cf. 1 Kings 19:10). His pain was unending; it was like a wound that would not heal. Discouraged, Jeremiah began to blame God for his troubles. He accused God of being like "a deceptive brook" (15:18; "as a liar," KJV). He inferred that God was deceitful and unreliable and like the streams in Palestine that overflow with water after a heavy rain or rush with water from the melting snows in the spring. But in the heat of summer, when their refreshing waters are really needed, these streams are completely dried up (cf. Job 6:15). This is the same prophet who earlier had called God "the spring of living water" (2:13). If Jeremiah believed God was like that, he was dangerously close to renouncing his prophetic ministry.

Though his reaction was quite human, Jeremiah clearly had gone beyond the bounds of what God would permit. The rebuke was stern. Jeremiah had earlier appealed to Judah to return to the Lord (see chaps. 3–4), but now God found it necessary to make the same appeal to Jeremiah: "If you repent, I will restore you" (15:19; "If you return, then I will restore you," NASB). Jeremiah must take the medicine he had prescribed for others. He must repent if he were to continue as the Lord's servant. A prophet must speak "worthy, not worthless, words" (15:19) to be God's "spokesman" (literally, "my mouth"; cf. 1:9; Exod. 4:16). Jeremiah's mission was to turn Judah to God. He was not to abandon his convictions and become like one of them. There could be no compromise.

If doubt remains that Jeremiah was renouncing his call, 15:20 makes it clear that God was renewing the call. Jeremiah was being given a second chance (cf. Jonah 3:1), for the words are almost identical with 1:18–19. Jeremiah could again become a fortified wall of bronze whom the people might fight, but they could not overcome him. Jeremiah's reply to God's rebuke is not recorded; but he did return to the Lord, for his prophetic ministry continued. Jeremiah's experience is a reminder that one is free to accept or to reject God's call, but once having accepted it, God expects obedience (cf. Luke 9:62; 14:26–35). The reward for faithful service may be rejection by one's friends and even harder service.

For Further Study

1. Of what possible benefit can hardship and persecution be to a Christian?

2. Why do the wicked prosper?

3. Is a servant of God ever justified in calling for divine vengeance on his enemies?

4. Is it possible for human nature to change?

5. Make a study of the various names of God found in the Old Testament.

Chapter 4

Further Crises in Jeremiah's Life
(Jeremiah 16:1–20:18)

Chapters 16–20 continue the intimate unveiling of the prophet's soul. The remaining "confessions" of Jeremiah are found in these chapters. Jeremiah's final "confession" (chap. 20) contains a shocking accusation against God and reveals abject despair that saw death as the only solution for his sufferings.

Though these outpourings of his heart are not dated, it is quite likely the events that triggered them occurred during the reign of King Jehoiakim. Jeremiah would not have experienced plots and open accusations earlier during the reign of Josiah. But Jehoiakim was a formidable adversary. From the beginning of his reign (cf. 26:1–11), the king's personal animosity encouraged others openly to seek Jeremiah's death. These difficult times probably were responsible for the "confessions" of Jeremiah.

A. Some Threats and Promises (16:1–21)

1. *Jeremiah forbidden to marry* (16:1–4)

The price for being a prophet of God is nowhere expressed more acutely than in the commands that required Jeremiah to sacrifice his own feelings and desires to God's purposes. The Lord forbade Jeremiah to marry and have a family (16:2; cf. Hosea, who was commanded to marry, Hos. 1:2). It was another of the symbolic acts (cf. 13:1) by which Jeremiah communicated God's messages to Judah. Whereas other symbolic acts might cause temporary inconveniences or embarrassment, this one denied Jeremiah a family as long as he lived.

In any age the suppression of the desire for a home and family could be a painful experience, but in Jeremiah's world it was even more difficult. The Jews understood that God wanted them to marry and have children (Gen. 1:28; 2:24). A man was expected to be married by the time he was eighteen or twenty; marriage at fourteen or fifteen was not uncommon. The Talmud says a man was cursed who did not marry by twenty! Children were considered a blessing, and the failure to have them was interpreted as a curse from God. Without children a man's property could not remain intact in the family, and his name would be forgotten by future generations.

Why, then, did the Lord, who established marriage, deny it to Jeremiah? Though it may be difficult for us to understand, a greater purpose was being served. Through abstinence from marriage, Jeremiah's life was a dramatic warning to Judah that judgment was imminent. It was no time to think about planning for family and home (cf. 1 Cor. 7:26). The Lord painted a bleak picture of children who would die of deadly diseases and by sword and famine. Why have children when they would soon die? In the coming siege of Jerusalem there would be no time for lamenting the dead or for burying them. Their bodies would become food for the birds and wild animals (16:4; cf. Deut. 28:26).

2. *Jeremiah forbidden to mourn or feast* (16:5–9)

Many commentators consider these verses to be a continuation of the preceding symbolic act. The meaning is much the same. The Lord told Jeremiah not to enter a house where death had taken a member of the family (16:5). The time was coming when the normal expressions of grief, such as a funeral meal, lamenting, cutting the flesh, and shaving the head, could not be observed. The latter was forbidden by Mosaic law, probably because of association with pagan religious rituals (Lev. 19:27–28; 21:5; Deut. 14:1). It was widely practiced in Jeremiah's time, however (41:4–5; Ezek. 7:18). Soon the bringing of food as an expression of comfort to those in mourning or the giving of something to drink for consolation could not be offered, not even for one's father or mother (16:7).

By forbidding Jeremiah to express grief for the dead, God was saying to Judah that the time was coming when He would show no grief for the people who would die in the time of calamity.

Further, God instructed Jeremiah not to enter a house where there was feasting and join the happy people who were eating and drinking (16:8). A time was coming when there would be no shouts of joy and merrymaking in Jerusalem. There would be no sound of the festivities associated with a marriage celebration when Jerusalem was under siege (16:9).

The injunction against Jeremiah's participation in the normal customs associated with family and communal life in Judah meant that he would be isolated socially from his kinsmen and friends. He could not mourn or feast with them. His antisocial behavior would gain him no friends in Judah. It was a heavy price to pay for being a prophet of God.

3. *Judah's sin will bring punishment* (16:10–13)

The Lord told Jeremiah to anticipate questions from the people of Judah. They would ask him why the Lord had decreed such a great disaster against them. They would ask what sin they had committed against God (16:10). It is unbelievable that a people who knew the covenant obligations imposed by the law upon them could ask these questions. But the answer to be given them was clear. Punishment was coming because their forefathers had forsaken God for other gods and had not kept the law (16:11).

However, punishment was not for the sins of previous generations (cf. Ezek. 18:2–4). The present generation was even worse, having done more evil than their forefathers. They followed the stubbornness of their evil hearts instead of obeying God (16:12). God was going to throw them out of the land (16:13; cf. 1 Sam. 18:11, where the verb describes Saul hurling a javelin; Jonah 1:4, where God hurled a storm into the sea). With a tinge of irony God promised to send them to a strange land where they could serve their other gods day and night (16:13). The warning reminds us that God sometimes allows us what we think we want, to our later sorrow.

4. *A promise of return from exile* (16:14–15)

A word of hope, placed between messages of judgment, is now sounded for the Israelites. As surely as God had delivered them from slavery in Egypt, He promised that He would return them to their land after a period of banishment. The words suggest a new Exodus, this time from Babylon, that would surpass the Egyptian Exodus. Again we are reminded that mingled messages of judgment and hope are characteristic of the prophets.

5. *No escape from punishment* (16:16–18)

Lest someone hearing Jeremiah's words of hope think he could escape the calamity, the message of judgment of 16:11–13 was resumed. The Lord warned that like fish being taken from the sea and like animals being ferreted out of their hiding places by hunters, so Judah's fugitives who sought to escape in the day of disaster would be hunted down and captured (16:16; cf. Amos 9:1–4). What they had done was not hidden from God (16:17). He was going to repay them double for their sin because they had polluted His land with their detestable idols (16:18; cf. Isa. 40:2).

6. *The power and might of God will be known* (16:19–21)

Jeremiah praised God as "my strength and my fortress, my refuge in time of distress" (16:19). In a statement interpreted as messianic, he spoke of a time when the nations from the ends of the earth will be converted. They will acknowledge that their gods are not really gods (16:19–20). The chapter closes with a brief expression of God's determination to make Judah know His power and might and to know that His name is "the LORD," i.e., He is all He claims to be—living and able to enforce His decrees (16:21; cf. 14:7 for significance of the "name").

B. Warnings and Exhortations (17:1–27)

This chapter is a collection of Jeremiah's messages that contain no single, unifying theme.

1. *Judah's indelible sin* (17:1–4)

Judah's sin problem could not be dealt with lightly, for her sin was deeply engraved on her heart, as though with a "flint point" (17:1; "diamond," KJV) of an iron stylus (cf. 31:33; Job 19:23–24). The Hebrew word *shamir* does not indicate a diamond, for this gem was unknown in biblical times. The word refers to a stone of impenetrable hardness; it also has been translated as adamant, emery, and corundum. Judah's sin was like an inscription carved into a rock surface with an iron tool. It was so deep-seated that it was even incised on the horns of the altar where the blood of the sin offering was smeared to remove sin (17:1; cf. Exod. 29:12; Lev. 4:7).

Their pagan altars and Asherah poles were everywhere. These poles were cult objects associated with the worship of the Canaanite goddess Asherah and were strictly forbidden (Deut. 16:21). Because their devotion to their altars and idols was so firmly established, God warned that their land would be despoiled of its wealth and the people would be led into captivity to serve their enemies. They had kindled God's anger by their sins, and it would burn forever (17:3–4).

2. A song of contrasts (17:5–8)

The rest of chapter 17 contrasts two ways to live. One way is to trust in man and to seek for life's solutions through the strength of the flesh. Today this is called humanism. That person will be like "a bush in the wastelands" (17:6; "desert," NASB), whose existence is only a desperate, barren quest for survival and meaning.

The other way is the life of trust in the Lord. That person is blessed. His life will be like a "tree planted by the water" (17:8; cf. Ps. 1:3), fruitful, without anxiety, stable, and able to withstand the difficult times ("when heat comes").

Jeremiah may have had in mind King Jehoiakim, who placed his confidence in an Egyptian alliance, or King Zedekiah, who did the same thing.

3. Deceitfulness of the human heart (17:9–10)

Jeremiah revealed the fallacy of trusting in other people: "The heart is deceitful above all things and beyond cure" (17:9; cf. Mark 7:21–22; Gal. 5:19–21). Jeremiah would have denied a popular belief of our day that man is basically good. The Bible everywhere affirms that we are sinners. The only remedy is radical transformation: "You must be born again" (John 3:7).

God searches every "heart" (the seat of reason and intelligence in Hebrew thought) and tests the "mind" (17:10; "reins," KJV). The Hebrew text has "kidneys" instead of "mind," for in Hebrew thought the kidneys were usually the equivalent of the conscience (12:2; "heart," NIV) or emotions (11:20; "feelings," NASB; cf. 20:12). As a result of this careful scrutiny God rewards or punishes each person according to what he or she has done.

4. Warning against ill-gotten wealth (17:11)

In order to warn the people against wealth acquired unjustly, Jeremiah quoted a well-known proverb (cf. 31:29): "Like a partridge that hatches eggs it did not lay is the man who gains riches by unjust means" (17:11). It was popularly believed that the partridge would hatch the eggs of other birds. However, when grown the alien brood would take wing and leave the mother, which they instinctively recognized as not their own. Possessions acquired unlawfully are just as precarious, and the security found in them will soon be gone.

5.   *The Lord as the hope of Israel* (17:12-13)

The fourth of Jeremiah's "confessions" is found in 17:12-18. It is uncertain whether the "confession" properly begins with verse 12 or verse 14.

Jeremiah shared the belief of his people that God's presence dwelt in the temple in Jerusalem. Therefore the sacred sanctuary was frequently called the throne of God (17:12; cf. 3:17; Ezek. 43:7). Because of Jeremiah's vigorous denunciation of the temple in 7:1-15, some wonder how he could now praise it. There is no conflict, however. In chapter 7 Jeremiah was condemning a false confidence in the temple; here he spoke of it in its relation to true believers, those who were holy and obedient.

Jeremiah proclaimed the Lord as the true hope of Israel (17:13; cf. 14:8). He warned that all who forsake Him will be put to shame. Those who turn away will be as impermanent as a name "written in the dust" (17:13). Their doom will be the result of having forsaken the Lord, the "spring of living water" (17:13; cf. 2:13).

6.   *Jeremiah's prayer for vindication* (17:14-18)

Having acknowledged the Lord as Israel's hope, Jeremiah then made a personal appeal for healing and salvation (17:14). The next verse reveals the cause for his plea. His enemies were taunting him that his dire predictions of doom and destruction had not come to pass. In their arrogant smugness they provoked the faithful prophet: "Where is the word of the LORD? Let it now be fulfilled!" (17:15; cf. 2 Peter 3:4).

When Jeremiah first preached his messages of judgment, the people might have been frightened by them. But years passed, and nothing happened. Jeremiah continued preaching the same message, but it was like hearing a broken record. Consequently, he had become an object of ridicule and scorn. Many concluded that he was a false prophet, for it appeared to them that he had failed to meet the test of the true prophet—his words had not come true (cf. Deut. 18:21-22).

Jeremiah reminded the Lord that he had been like a faithful shepherd (17:16; the only time the word is used of a prophet) in his proclamation of God's warnings, though he himself did not desire the day of judgment. He had spoken God's words; but by so doing, he had become an object of ridicule to his people. He turned to God as his only refuge (17:17).

As in each of the other "confessions," Jeremiah then called on God to vindicate him by punishing his persecutors (17:18). Jeremiah was not content with a slap on the wrist. He insisted that God crush them with "double destruction," i.e., complete obliteration! Jeremiah's cry for vengeance cannot be defended, but it serves as another reminder that the prophets were human.

7. *The importance of Sabbath observance* (17:19–27)

The Sabbath has always been one of the most important religious practices of the Jewish people. Its observance through the centuries has been given credit by some for the survival of the Jewish people. Its origin is embedded in the Mosaic law (Exod. 20:8–11; cf. Deut. 5:12–15). The manner in which it should be observed has consumed countless hours of discussion and disputation among the interpreters of the Law through the centuries.

The Lord told Jeremiah to go and stand at "the gate of the people" (17:19). This gate is called "Benjamin Gate" by the RSV, but it cannot be identified with certainty; it was probably a gate into the temple. The prophet also was to go to all the other gates of Jerusalem and preach concerning the Sabbath observance. The people were told that they should not carry a load on the Sabbath, either out of the houses or through the gates of Jerusalem. They were not to do any work on the Sabbath, but they had refused to obey (17:21–23).

If they carefully observed the Sabbath, the Lord promised to bless them. Kings would continue to sit on the throne of David, and Jerusalem would be inhabited forever (17:25). People would come from other cities, bringing their offerings and sacrifices to the temple (17:26). However, if they did not keep the Sabbath holy by refraining from work, God would destroy Jerusalem (17:27). The message was clear: national survival depended on proper Sabbath observance.

C. Lessons from the Potter (18:1–19:15)

Jeremiah's visit to the potter is one of the best-known narratives in the book. Another of the symbolic acts (cf. 13:1), its immediate purpose was to warn of coming judgment, but its theological implications still provoke discussion.

1. *Jeremiah's visit to the potter* (18:1–12)

The Lord instructed Jeremiah to go to the potter's house and observe him at work (18:2).[1] It was a familiar activity throughout the ancient Near East and one Jeremiah had witnessed many times. He saw the potter place the moist lump of clay on a revolving wheel (literally, "two stones"). Then with deft and skillful hands the potter shaped it. Occasionally, the vessel did not assume the desired form. Instead of throwing the lump of clay away, the potter patiently reworked it into the desired shape (18:4).

As Jeremiah watched the familiar process, God spoke to him and compared Himself to a potter (18:6; cf. Isa. 29:16; 45:9; 64:8; Rom. 9:19–24). Israel was like a lump of clay in His hands to be formed as He desired. God could destroy a wicked nation or spare it if it reformed. A nation that was blessed by Him could have its blessings withdrawn by disobedience (18:7–10).

Jeremiah was to speak to the people and warn them that God was "preparing" a disaster against His people (18:11; "shaping," RSV, *Moffatt;* from the same word as "potter"; the verb means "to form" or "to shape"). At the same time He appealed to them to turn from their evil ways. However, He already knew what their reply would be: "It's no use" (18:12; "It's hopeless," NASB). They would continue with their own plans and follow the stubbornness of their evil hearts. The warnings fell on deaf ears.

The message contained in Jeremiah's symbolic visit to the potter was clear: Destruction was coming if the people did not repent. There are important theological principles implied in the visit. It teaches the sovereignty of God; like the potter's right over the lump of clay, God could do whatever He wanted with Israel. Parallel to this teaching are the implications of the grace of God and of His patience. The potter might have thrown the marred piece of clay away; instead, he continued working with it to mold it into the desired shape. God could have made a permanent break with Israel the first time she violated the covenant. Instead, He patiently continued both by blessing and chastisement through many centuries to try to make her into the kind of

---

[1]See James L. Kelso, "The Ceramic Vocabulary of the Old Testament," *Bulletin of the American Schools of Oriental Research, Supplementary Studies*, Nos. 5 and 6 (New Haven: American Schools of Oriental Research, 1948): 9–10; and Elmer A. Leslie, *Jeremiah* (New York: Abingdon Press, 1954), pp. 191–92, for descriptions of the potter and his work.

people who would bring honor to His name. The story of Jeremiah's visit also teaches that God deals with us on the basis of the moral choices we make.

Finally, the passage reminds us that prophetic utterances are sometimes conditional, whether stated or implied. "If" is the key word by which a conditional prophecy may be recognized (18:8, 10). The condition may be implied, however, as when Jonah announced the destruction of Nineveh in forty days (Jonah 3:4). Prophetic passages in the Bible may be misinterpreted if the conditional element is overlooked.

2. The unnaturalness of Israel's sin (18:13–17)

The unnaturalness of Judah's rejection of God is a frequent theme of Jeremiah (cf. 2:11, 32; 5:22–23; 8:7). There were no parallels among the heathen for Judah's faithlessness (18:13).

Though the Hebrew of verse 14 is difficult, the verse probably means that it was unnatural for the snow of Lebanon to vanish from its rocky slopes or its cool waters to cease flowing. It was equally unnatural that the Lord's people had forgotten Him. They offered incense to worthless idols. They had turned from the "ancient paths" (18:15; probably a reference to the covenant that had been broken; cf. 6:16). Therefore, they could expect the curses of a broken covenant to fall on them (18:16–17). That they would deliberately turn their back on God and incur His wrath was unnatural and inexplicable.

3. A plot against Jeremiah (18:18–23)

A plot against Jeremiah prompted the fifth of his "confessions" and his most violent appeal for vengeance on his enemies. An earlier plot had been directed against his life (11:18–23), but this one was aimed at his reputation. His enemies said to one another, "Let's attack him with our tongues" (18:18). They determined to denounce him openly as a false prophet for claiming that the teaching of the law by the priest would come to an end or that the giving of counsel by the wise men or words of the prophets would cease (18:18). Jeremiah knew that all these institutions would end in the forthcoming destruction, but the people vehemently denied that his dire predictions would come to pass.

Almost petulantly Jeremiah insisted that God pay attention to him and listen to what his enemies were saying (18:19). His intentions had been good. His only desire was to avert the terrible calamity that was coming, but his good was repaid by evil (18:20). Was this any way to repay a faithful prophet?

The strain was too much for Jeremiah. He had reached the end of his patience with his countrymen. In an outburst unprecedented for a prophet, Jeremiah called on God to pour out His wrath on them. He demanded no mercy for men, women, or children. He wanted all of them to experience famine and the sword (18:21–22).

Jeremiah's violent demand for punishment was not based on a desire to defend God's honor. It was totally personal: "For they have dug a pit to capture me and have hidden snares for my feet" (18:22). But Jeremiah's rage was not yet abated. He demanded that God not forgive their iniquity or ever blot out their sin from His sight. Moreover, he asked that God not deal with them in a time of calm reflection but punish them when He was angry (18:23)! This is the prophet who earlier interceded with tears for God to spare these people.

To read this "confession" is painful and almost embarrassing. It shatters the image of an "other worldly" prophet who endures the most outrageous treatment without a word of protest. It would have been sufficient to leave judgment to the Lord to bring it about as He saw fit. But, having reached a breaking point, Jeremiah was dictating to God the kind of punishment he wanted inflicted on his enemies.

The curses, or imprecations, on one's enemies found in the Old Testament (e.g., Pss. 35:4–8; 40:14–15; 54:5; 55:15; 58:6–8; 69:19–28; 83:9–18; 109; 129:5–6; 137; 143; but cf. Prov. 24:17) must not serve as proof texts for dealing with one's enemies. However, "All scripture is God-breathed and is useful for teaching" (2 Tim. 3:16). Jeremiah's outburst must be understood as an instructive example of how a Christian should *not* respond to personal abuse. The New Testament pattern for a Christian's response is found in Matthew 5:44; 6:14–15; Romans 12:19; Ephesians 4:32. Jeremiah's reaction was completely human, but it was equally wrong. Perhaps he was seeing sin as God does and was pronouncing God's judgment on it, as some say; but he assumed a judgmental prerogative that was not his.

That Jeremiah's outburst did not merit a response from the Lord is verified by the absence of a recorded answer.

4. A *broken clay jar* (19:1–15)

Chapters 18 and 19 share the common theme of the potter. The first focuses on the making of a clay jar, and the second on its use as a symbolic act. In 20:1–6 we read of the sufferings endured by Jeremiah as a result of these messages.

The Lord instructed Jeremiah to purchase a clay jar (19:1; from an onomatopoeic word, *baqbuq*, that suggests the sound of water being poured out). Then he was to assemble some of the elders and priests and take them to the Valley of Ben Hinnom (cf. 7:31) at the entrance of the "Potsherd Gate" (19:2; "east gate," KJV; the exact location is unknown, but it may have been near the section of the city where potters worked and near the dump where broken and defective pottery was discarded). There in their presence he was to proclaim the Lord's words that would be told him. They would be words of impending calamity because Judah had forsaken God for other gods and because the people had offered human sacrifice (19:4). Their children were being given as burnt offerings to Baal, something God had never ordered or even considered (19:5).

The time would come when the valley would no longer be called Topheth (cf. 7:31) but the Valley of Slaughter (19:6; cf. 7:32). In that place God would "ruin" (19:7; literally, "pour out," from the same word as "jar," 19:1) the plans of Judah and Jerusalem. The inhabitants would fall by the sword of their enemies and serve as food for the birds and wild animals. Jerusalem would be so devastated that people would be amazed and "scoff" (19:8; "hiss," NASB; a gesture of derision or surprise) when they saw it (cf. Lam. 2:15–16). The siege would become so desperate that people would be reduced to cannibalism, eating their own children (19:9; cf. Deut. 28:53; Lam. 4:10).

After proclaiming these words Jeremiah was instructed by the Lord to smash the clay jar before his audience to symbolize the coming destruction of Jerusalem (19:10–11). The smashing of the jar symbolized the unloosing of a curse on the city. God was determined to make Jerusalem just as defiled as Topheth because of its worship practices directed to other gods.

After carrying out the symbolic act according to the instructions given him, Jeremiah returned to the court of the temple (19:14). There he warned all the people that calamity was coming on Jerusalem and Judah because they had stubbornly refused to listen to the Lord's words (19:15).

D. Jeremiah's Punishment and Despair (20:1–18)

The sixth and final of Jeremiah's "confessions" is found in this chapter. It contains his bitterest complaint of all and has sometimes been called his Gethsemane. The first six verses describe the circumstances that probably led to the prophet's anguished outcry. The rest of the chapter is the "confession" itself.

1. *Pashhur's violent reaction to Jeremiah's warnings (20:1-6)*

Pashhur, the chief officer in the temple, heard Jeremiah's pronouncements of doom on Jerusalem. He reacted by ordering Jeremiah beaten. Then he had him "put in stocks at the Upper Gate of Benjamin at the LORD's temple" to be made a spectacle and object of ridicule to all who passed by (20:2; cf. 37:13; 38:7; Acts 16:24).

When Pashhur released him the next day, Jeremiah gave him a new name. He said, "The LORD's name for you is not Pashhur, but Magor-Missabib" (i.e., "terror on every side," 20:3; cf. Lam. 2:22). The name meant that Pashhur would become a terror to himself and to all his friends. He would see some of them perish by the sword of their enemies. Others would be carried as exiles to Babylon (20:4; Jeremiah's first specific mention of Babylon as the place of exile), and the wealth and treasures of the city would be plundered and carried away (20:5). Pashhur himself and all his family would be taken as captives to Babylon where he and all his friends would die (20:6). The priest would receive this punishment because he had acted as a false prophet (cf. 28:15-16; Amos 7:17; 2 Peter 2:1).

2. *The prophet's lament (20:7-18)*

Whether the words of the "confession" were spoken immediately after Jeremiah's release cannot be determined, but they fit well the mood of despair he surely felt at that time.

a) *The depths of despair (20:7-10)*

Jeremiah had received nothing but ridicule, threats, and physical abuse for faithfully preaching God's messages. These messages would have saved Judah from destruction, had she heeded them.

With Pashhur's humiliating treatment, Jeremiah finally reached the depths of despair. No previous complaint had been so bitter, and none like it would be heard from his lips again. He began abruptly with an accusation directed to God: "O LORD, you deceived me, and I was deceived" (20:7). The word "deceived" is the same word found in Exodus 22:16, where it means to seduce a young woman. The intensive form of the verb further indicates Jeremiah's extreme state of emotional agitation.

He continued the comparison of his experience to seduction by saying God had forced him to be a prophet against his will. He accused, "You overpowered me and prevailed" (20:7). Such blasphemous language has its nearest parallel in accusations made by a beleaguered Job against God (Job 16:7–14). Being the prophet of God had not brought honor and respect, only mockery and ridicule; so now Jeremiah was blaming God for his woes.

He complained that God limited his preaching to messages of doom, saying, "I cry out proclaiming violence and destruction" (20:8). He tried to keep silent to avoid the insults and derision of his detractors, but he quickly discovered that the word was in his heart "like a burning fire, shut up in my bones" (20:9). He became "weary of holding it in," and in fact he could not. Jeremiah wanted to stop preaching in order to protect himself but could not! He had to speak. No other passage in the Bible reveals quite so clearly the divine compulsion to speak for God (cf. 5:14; 6:11; Amos 3:8; 1 Cor. 9:16).

Jeremiah heard his enemies whispering to one another that all he could speak about was "Terror on every side!" (20:10). This perhaps was a nickname given to him, the same name he had transferred to Pashhur (20:3). His trusted friends (literally, "every man of my peace") were denouncing him and waiting for him to slip so they could prevail against him and take their revenge (20:10).

b) A momentary regaining of confidence (20:11–13)

In the midst of his dark mood Jeremiah remembered that the Lord was with him "like a mighty warrior" (20:11). A psychologist might say Jeremiah was beginning to practice positive thinking! He took comfort that his persecutors would stumble and not prevail against him. He was sure that they would be disgraced and that their dishonor would never be forgotten (20:11). Then he appealed to the Lord, as he had done in all his "confessions," to bring vengeance on his enemies (20:12). By this time the earlier mood of despair had been replaced by euphoria, and for a moment Jeremiah felt reassured that God was with him. "Sing to the LORD! Give praise to the LORD!" was his jubilant cry (20:13).

c) A curse on his day of birth (20:14–18)

It cannot be known whether these words immediately followed

Jeremiah's mood of exaltation or whether some time elapsed. However, anyone who has experienced a spiritual crisis would have no difficulty believing that a person could be praising God in one breath and in the next wishing he had never been born!

The birth of a baby in Israel was a joyful occasion not only for the parents but for the entire community. It was viewed as an evidence of God's favor on the family. However, at the moment, Jeremiah did not view the day of his birth as a happy occasion. He pronounced a curse on the day (20:14; cf. Job 3:1–3) and a curse on the person who brought the news of his birth to his father (20:15–16; ordinarily that person was rewarded for being the bearer of good news). He even expressed a desire that his life might have been snuffed out while he was still in his mother's womb (20:17).

Jeremiah must have remembered the fifth commandment (Exod. 20:12) and could not bring himself to curse his parents. This was as close to breaking the commandment as he dared come. Jeremiah wished he had never been born because life had brought him so much trouble and sorrow. He could only anticipate that he would come to the end of his days in shame (20:18).

Here the "confession" ended. We are not told whether God rebuked Jeremiah (as He did earlier in 15:19–21) or whether He mercifully ignored the complaints. Nor are we told how long his state of depression and despair continued. But Jeremiah must have emerged from the furnace of affliction and self-doubt a stronger person. There must have come a time when he could say like Job, "When he has tested me, I will come forth as gold" (Job 23:10), for never again do we hear complaints or "confessions" of a tortured soul that characterized Jeremiah up to this moment. He became the "fortified city, an iron pillar and a bronze wall" (1:18) that God said he would be. He faced death on more than one occasion but faithfully continued preaching, "This is what the LORD says," till last heard from in the land of Egypt (44:30).

Some lessons can be learned from Jeremiah's "confessions" of chapters 11–20: (1) prophets are human beings; (2) a true servant of God may have times of difficulty doing the will of God; (3) we need not be ashamed to admit our weaknesses and doubts to God; (4) the acknowledgment of our weaknesses may serve to encourage someone else that there is hope for him; (5) God uses very human, imperfect people to carry out His work.

For Further Study

1. In a Bible dictionary or encyclopedia (see bibliography) read articles on: marriage, Asherah, Sabbath, Topheth, and curses.

2. Make a study of the significance of names in the ancient Near East.

3. What lessons can be learned from Jeremiah's visit to the potter?

4. How do you explain Jeremiah's frequent requests to God to bring vengeance on his enemies?

Chapter 5

Messages Concerning Judah and the Nations
(Jeremiah 21:1–25:38)

Jeremiah's concern for his people was deep and genuine. His heart was broken (23:9) because of the wickedness of Judah that was leading the nation to destruction. But Jeremiah's ministry was not limited to his own people. He had been called as a prophet to the nations (1:5), and so he proclaimed that the cup of wrath (25:16) was not only for Judah but for all nations. By faith he knew that the Lord his God was the only true God and that His reign and authority were universal.

A. Prophecies Against the Kings of Judah (21:1–22:30)

Jeremiah's ministry spanned the reigns of five of Judah's kings. With the exception of Josiah, Jeremiah preached messages against all these kings. Some of these messages were collected and arranged together in chapters 21–22. Their placement here serves as another reminder that the Book of Jeremiah was not arranged in a strictly chronological sequence from beginning to end.

1. A reply to Zedekiah's inquiry (21:1–10)

During the siege of Jerusalem by Nebuchadnezzar[1] that began in 588 B.C., King Zedekiah sent an inquiry to Jeremiah by Pashhur (not the Pashhur of 20:1; cf. 38:1) and Zephaniah (not the prophet; cf. 29:25; 37:3; 52:24; Zeph. 1:1). So far as is known, it was the first time Jeremiah

---

[1]This is the first mention of this ruler by name in the Book of Jeremiah. The Hebrew of this verse uses the spelling Nebuchadrezzar, which is closer to the Babylonian spelling. However, the more familiar "Nebuchadnezzar" will be used throughout this study. The name is thought to mean "May Nebo protect the boundary stone." Recently it has been argued that spelled "–nezzar" it means "May Nebo protect the mule" as a Hebrew way of ridiculing the Babylonian ruler.

was consulted at the initiative of the king (cf. 37:3–10). Zedekiah wanted Jeremiah to ask God if He was going to perform a miracle ("wonders," 21:2) that would cause the enemy to withdraw. Perhaps he remembered Jerusalem's deliverance from Assyrian destruction when Hezekiah was king (2 Kings 19:6–7, 32–36; cf. Isa. 7:14–16; 2 Kings 6:8–23; 7:1–7). God had delivered His people from their enemies many times in the past. There was precedent to believe He would do it again, notwithstanding Judah's wickedness.

However, Jeremiah quickly dispelled any false hopes of the king. He sent word to Zedekiah that not only was the city going to be taken but that God Himself was going to fight against Jerusalem (21:5). Many in the city would die of a terrible plague. Zedekiah and others who survived the siege would be taken by Nebuchadnezzar, who would show them no pity (21:7).

Jeremiah did offer a way by which the nation could escape destruction. He set before her "the way of life and the way of death" (21:8; cf. Deut. 30:15–20; Josh. 24:15; 1 Kings 18:21; Ps. 1). Those who chose to remain in Jerusalem would die by sword, famine, or plague. However, those who would surrender to the Babylonians (literally, Chaldeans, the inhabitants of a region in southern Babylonia; the name was later applied to all Babylonia) would escape with their lives (21:9). Nothing would deter God from destroying Jerusalem, but those who would obey and surrender would be spared. It was a choice that seemed illogical, but faith does not always seem logical by human standards. Jeremiah was probably called a traitor for suggesting such a course of action.

2. A message against the house of the king of Judah (21:11–12)

Jeremiah appealed to the royal house of Judah to administer justice and to deliver the oppressed so that God's wrath would not go forth like fire against the land. Jeremiah shared the same concern for the oppressed as did Amos and other prophets.

3. A message against Jerusalem (21:13–14)

David chose well when he made Jerusalem his capital (2 Sam. 5:6–9). Because of its location on a narrow ridge and its massive city walls, it could be easily defended. However, its inhabitants had a false sense of confidence that no enemy could pierce the defenses of the city (21:13; cf. Obad. 3). God informed them that because He was against them, the city was not secure. He was going to kindle a fire in it that would destroy it (21:14).

4. A message to the king and the city (22:1-9)

The Lord sent Jeremiah to the house of the king of Judah (probably Zedekiah) to exhort him and all the people to act justly and with righteousness. The appeal was also made to the king to deliver the oppressed, not to mistreat strangers (i.e., resident aliens), orphans, and widows, nor to shed innocent blood (22:3). The Lord promised that if they would do these things, kings would continue to sit on David's throne (22:4). But He swore by Himself (no more solemn or binding oath could be taken; cf. Gen. 22:16; Isa. 45:23) that if they did not obey, the royal house would become a ruin and as desolate as a desert (22:5-6).

The destruction would be so complete that travelers passing that way would ask why Judah's God had destroyed such a great city (22:8). The answer would be that the people had forsaken the covenant and were serving other gods (22:9).

5. A message against Shallum (22:10-12)

Upon the death of Josiah in 609 his son Shallum was placed on the throne. Shallum is listed fourth among Josiah's family in 1 Chronicles 3:15, but other Scriptures indicate he was older than Zedekiah (cf. 2 Kings 23:31 and 2 Chron. 36:11). He had another name, Jehoahaz, for kings frequently had a throne name and a personal name. Shallum was probably supported by Pharaoh Neco, whose troops controlled the region at the time. He reigned only three months before being deposed by the Egyptians, probably for disloyalty. He was taken captive to Egypt, where he died (2 Kings 23:31-34). These verses preserve a brief lament for the deposed king. Judah was exhorted not to weep for the dead (undoubtedly a reference to Josiah and, with 22:15-16, Jeremiah's only recorded comment about him). Instead, they should weep for Shallum, who had been taken to Egypt, for he would never return to his own land (22:10-12). Josiah's death in battle was not so tragic an end as his son's fate.

6. A message against Jehoiakim (22:13-19)

Shallum was succeeded by his older brother Eliakim, whose name was changed to Jehoiakim (2 Kings 23:34; 2 Chron. 36:4). He was another son of Josiah. Jehoiakim gave allegiance to Pharaoh until Nebuchadnezzar defeated the Egyptians at Carchemish in 605. Then he transferred his allegiance to Babylonia but rebelled against Nebuchadnezzar three years later. The Babylonian ruler sent an army to quell the rebellion. What followed is uncertain, but Jehoiakim died (perhaps killed by his own courtiers in order to make peace with Nebuchadnezzar); and his son Jehoiachin came to the throne (2 Kings 23:35–24:7).

Jehoiakim was an unrelenting adversary of Jeremiah. He refused to take any of the prophet's advice. The animosity was mutual, for Jeremiah had no respect for the wicked king. He pronounced woe on one who would build his dynasty without righteousness or justice. He condemned him for forcing his people to work for him without wages (22:13; cf. Solomon, 1 Kings 5:13–14; 12:3–4, 18). His vanity led him to build a magnificent palace that was paneled with cedar and painted bright red inside (22:14). Jeremiah sarcastically asked him if trying to outdo other rulers by an ostentatious building program made him a king (22:15).

Buildings would not make Jehoiakim a great king. He should have done what was "right and just" like his father Josiah; then he could have expected all to go well with him (22:15). Defending the cause of the poor and needy was the best demonstration of what it meant to know God (22:16).

However, because Jehoiakim's heart was set only on dishonest gain, the shedding of innocent blood, oppression, and extortion (22:17), there would be no mourning for him when he died (22:18). He would be buried like a donkey—dragged away and thrown outside the gates of Jerusalem (22:19). The record of Jehoiakim's actual death says he "rested with his fathers" (2 Kings 24:6), which is the usual way of speaking of a peaceful death and burial. Was Jeremiah's prediction incorrect? The answer is that Jehoiakim probably did receive proper burial, but later his body was disinterred and his bones scattered by the Babylonians or by his own people (cf. 8:1–2).

7. A message against Jerusalem (22:20–23)

The Lord reminded Jerusalem that He had warned her when she felt secure, but she would not listen (22:21). Since she had never obeyed His voice, judgment was coming that would bring shame and disgrace to the proud city. The wind would drive away their shepherds (22:22), i.e., leaders; literally, the text says "the wind will shepherd your shepherds," a play on words. Their pain at the time of destruction would be like that of a woman in childbirth (22:23).

8. *Messages against Jehoiachin* (22:24-30)

Jehoiachin (also called Jeconiah and Coniah; cf. NIV margins of 1 Chron. 3:16-17 and Jer. 37:1) succeeded his father Jehoiakim as king but ruled for only three months (2 Kings 24:8-15). He quickly made peace with Nebuchadnezzar, and Jerusalem was spared the horrors of siege and destruction at that time. Carried into captivity, he remained in prison until released by Nebuchadnezzar's successor, Amel-Marduk (Evil-Merodach of 52:31-34) in 561 B.C.

Jeremiah had no encouragement for Jehoiachin during his brief reign. Even if he were God's signet ring (a most intimate personal possession and a symbol of authority), he would be removed and given to the Babylonians (22:24-25). He and his mother would both go into exile (22:26). He would be childless and would not prosper. He would have no offspring who would actually sit on the throne (22:30). This does not mean he would be childless in an absolute sense, for 1 Chronicles 3:17-18 records that Jehoiachin the captive had seven children. Zerubbabel, a grandson (1 Chron. 3:19), was one of the leaders of the return from exile, though not as king (Ezra 2:2; 3:2). Thus the prediction can be interpreted as meaning Jehoiachin was childless so far as having a son to rule after him.

B. Restoration and Ideal Rulers (23:1-8)

1. *Unworthy shepherds to be replaced by God's shepherds* (23:1-4)

Jeremiah understood that Judah's leaders were responsible for her predicament. The prophet called them "shepherds" (23:1), a word frequently used in the Bible and the ancient Near East for rulers (cf. 25:34-38; Ezek. 34; John 10). By their acts they were destroying and scattering the sheep of God's pasture and thus doing the exact opposite of what was expected of a shepherd. Because they had not tended the sheep faithfully, God was going to punish them (23:2). Then by a new Exodus He would bring His scattered flock back to the land where they would be fruitful and increase in number (23:3). The Lord Himself was going to set shepherds over them who would tend them and protect them from all danger (23:4).

2. The ideal king (23:5-8)

"The days are coming" (an expression found fifteen times in Jeremiah), declared the Lord, when He would raise up from David's line a righteous "Branch" (23:5). "Branch" is from a word meaning "to grow" or "sprout"; the term is used elsewhere in the ancient Near East to refer to the rightful heir to the throne (33:15; Isa. 4:2; Zech. 3:8; 6:12; cf. Isa. 11:1 where a different Hebrew word is used). He would be a king who would act wisely and do what was just and right (23:5). During his reign "Judah will be saved and Israel will live in safety" and "he will be called: The LORD Our Righteousness" (23:6). The latter name was perhaps spoken as a wordplay on the name Zedekiah, which means "The Lord is righteous" (cf. 3:17; 33:16; Ezek. 48:35; 1 Cor. 1:30).

The passage is clearly messianic and was one of many such utterances by the prophets that contributed to the developing messianic belief in ancient Israel. The other principal messianic statements of Jeremiah are found in 30:8-9, 21; 33:15-16 (cf. Luke 24:27).

As surely as the Lord delivered Israel from Egypt, there would be a second Exodus by which He would bring her again into her own land. People would no longer talk about the first Exodus because the second would be so much greater (23:7-8).

C. Messages Against False Prophets (23:9-40)

The people of Judah were not thinking clearly; they believed that Jeremiah was a false prophet and that those prophets who continually assured them that all was well were the true prophets. Even after Jerusalem's fall, when Jeremiah was vindicated as a true prophet, the people still did not listen to him (cf. 43:2). They did not see that his attempts to expose the false prophets were motivated not by desire for recognition, but by a concern for the nation that faced a calamity.

1. Wickedness in the land (23:9-12)

As Jeremiah considered what the false prophets were doing, his heart was broken (23:9). He was overwhelmed by the sin in the land. The Lord's holy words of judgment that were being ignored agitated him so much that he trembled and swayed like a drunken man (23:9). The Deuteronomic curse had fallen on the land because of the people's unfaithfulness to God (Deut. 28:23-24). Drought had dried up the pastures (23:10; "the land mourns," NASB; cf. 14:1–6). Ironically, Baal, the storm god whom they credited for supplying the rain, had failed them. The land was parched because they refused to acknowledge that the Lord, not Baal, was the source of their blessings.

Both prophet and priest were godless; evidence of their wickedness was found even in the temple (23:11; cf. Ezek. 8). They were on a slippery path and would be banished to darkness as God's punishment (23:12; cf. Ps. 35:6).

2. The evil prophets of Jerusalem (23:13–15)

The Lord compared the prophets of Jerusalem and Samaria (the capital of the northern kingdom of Israel, taken by Assyria in 722 B.C.). What God saw in Samaria was repulsive (literally, "tasteless," "empty"). Israel's prophets had prophesied by Baal and led that kingdom astray (23:13). But what God saw in Jerusalem was horrible. The prophets there were worse because they professed to serve the Lord but led immoral lives. They committed adultery (religious or physical?) and lied. They encouraged evildoers so that no one had a desire to turn from his wickedness (23:14).

The prophets had become to the Lord like Sodom and the people like Gomorrah (23:14). These two cities were synonymous with everything that was depraved and wicked in biblical times (Gen. 18:20–19:29; cf. Matt. 10:15; 2 Peter 2:6; Jude 7). Jerusalem was no different from those ancient cesspools of iniquity. For their part in leading Judah astray, the prophets would "eat bitter food and drink poisoned water" (23:15; cf. 9:15 for explanation of the phrase).

3. The message of the false prophets (23:16–22)

These verses describe the nature of the messages preached by the false prophets. Their messages were not from God and thus gave false hope to the people. Judah was warned not to listen to them because their visions came from their own minds, not from the mouth of the Lord (23:16). Their messages were giving false assurance to the people. To those in Judah who despised the Lord, the false prophets claimed that the Lord was promising peace to them (23:17). They assured those who followed the stubbornness of their hearts that no harm would come to them (23:17).

Their messages did not cause the people to turn away from their evil practices because the false prophets had not stood in the council of the

Lord[2] to hear His Word. If they had, they would have been preaching His words to the people (23:18, 22). The words they preached did not rebuke the people or lead them to repentance; rather, they encouraged them to continue in their wicked ways. God's wrath on such people would be like a storm, a whirlwind swirling down on their heads (23:19; cf. 30:23–24). God did not send them or give them messages to speak, but they prophesied anyway (23:21).

4. *Dreams of the false prophets* (23:23–32)

The false prophets must have believed that their evil deeds were hidden from God. Therefore, He warned them that He was not just a "God nearby" (23:23), a localized deity with limited power, one who was unable to be in faraway places. He was the God of the whole universe and could see everything. No one could hide himself from God (23:24). The false prophets might deceive the people, but God knew who they were and what they were doing.

To demonstrate the fact that He knew what the false prophets were doing, the Lord said He had heard the prophets who were claiming to have revelatory dreams (23:25). Their mysticism may have impressed their audiences, but they were prophesying out of the delusion of their own minds (23:26). They believed that their dreams would make the people forget God's name, i.e., His attributes and His character (cf. 14:7), just as their forefathers had forgotten His name because of their attraction to Baal (23:27).

With a touch of irony the Lord told the false prophets to go ahead and relate their dreams (for they were going to, anyway). However, He added that those who truly had His word should speak it in truth (23:28; cf. 1 Cor. 14:19). The difference in the prophets' dreams and God's word would be as great as the difference between straw and grain (23:28). God's word was like the grain that gives nourishment. It was also like fire and like a hammer that could shatter a rock (23:29; cf. Heb. 4:12). God's words had a totally different quality from the soothing words of the false prophets.

God warned that He was against the prophets who stole words from one another claiming that they were His words (23:30). Not having revelation of their own, they proclaimed as theirs what had been said by others. God was against those prophets who wagged their own

---

[2]There are other references in the Old Testament to a heavenly council. The most extended description is found in Job 1–2; 15:8 (cf. 1 Kings 22:19–22; Pss. 82:1; 89:7).

tongues and yet said that their words were the Lord's (23:31). He was against those who prophesied their false dreams, for they were leading the people away by their lies. God had not sent them, and they were not benefiting the people in the least (23:32).

It should be added that sometimes God used dreams to convey messages (cf. Gen. 37:5–10; Num. 12:6; 1 Sam. 28:6; Joel 2:28; Matt. 1:20). Dreams are condemned in Jeremiah 23:32 because they were not from God and were leading the people astray. The word of God was a sure guide, for it is truth.

5. *The burden of the Lord* (23:33–40)

The Lord instructed Jeremiah that when the people, or prophet, or priest asked him, "What is the oracle of the LORD?" he should answer, "What oracle?" (23:33).[3] Though the meaning of the dialogue is not quite clear, it serves to introduce a warning against claiming to have a message from God when one does not, whether prophet, priest, or anyone else (23:34). If they continued claiming oracles from the Lord, He would forget them and remove them from His presence, even as He was going to destroy Jerusalem (23:39). Their disgrace and shame would never be forgotten (23:40).

D. Vision of Two Baskets of Figs (24:1–10)

Jeremiah's vision of two baskets of figs occurred after 597 B.C., when Nebuchadnezzar carried Jehoiachin into captivity (2 Kings 24:15). There is some uncertainty whether the experience should be understood as visionary or whether Jeremiah actually saw two baskets of figs in front of the temple, perhaps placed there as an offering (cf. the visions of 1:11–14 and Amos 8:1–3).

One basket contained very good figs, the eagerly sought first ripe figs of the season. The other contained very bad figs, ("very naughty," KJV, but obviously archaic language!), so rotten they could not be eaten (24:2). As Jeremiah looked at the two baskets, the Lord enabled him to see them as representative of the exiles and those who remained in Jerusalem. The good figs represented those who would be taken into

---

[3]The Hebrew words for "oracle" and "burden" come from the same word that means "to lift up." The LXX and Vulgate therefore translate 23:33 as "If this people . . . should ask, What is the burden of the Lord, then you will say to them, 'You are the burden . . .'" When people would ask Jeremiah sarcastically what burdensome message from the Lord he had that day for them, he would retort by calling them the Lord's burden.

exile to Babylon (24:5). One day the Lord would bring them back to the land and build them up and plant them securely there (24:6; cf. 1:10; 18:9; 31:28). He would give them a heart to know Him, and they would return to Him wholeheartedly (24:7; cf. 31:33; Deut. 30:6; Ezek. 11:19; 36:26).

The bad figs represented Zedekiah, his officials, and others who remained in the land, as well as those who had fled to Egypt (24:8). They would become abhorrent and an offense to all the kingdoms of the earth, objects of ridicule and cursing wherever God would banish them (24:9). Any who remained in the land would be victims of sword, famine, and plague (24:10).

When Jehoiachin and others were taken to Babylon, those remaining probably said, "We are the choice figs, and you exiles are the bad figs that God has discarded." They felt superior to those who had been led away. However, God's ways are higher than our ways, and His thoughts higher than ours (Isa. 55:9). The future lay with the exiles, not with those who remained. Those taken captive would form the remnant that would return and rebuild the nation. They would be spared the terrible hardships endured by those who stayed in Judah.

E. God's Wrath Against Israel and the Nations (25:1–38)

The events of chapter 25 precede those of chapter 24 (cf. 25:1, 3 with 24:1) and serve as another reminder that the messages of the book are not always arranged chronologically.

1. Judah's continued disobedience (25:1-7)

It was the fourth year of the reign of Jehoiakim (605 B.C.), the same year Jeremiah dictated his messages to Baruch (cf. 36:4, 32). It was also the first year of the reign of Nebuchadnezzar, who had succeeded his father Nabopolassar as king of Babylon. Jeremiah had been preaching for twenty-three years, but the people of Judah had not received his messages as from God (25:1, 3). His tenacity was remarkable in view of the discouraging lack of response from his hearers. Other prophets had been sent, but they had not been heeded either. Their messages had not been essentially different from Jeremiah's—"Turn from your wickedness and abandon your idols, and God will bless you" (cf. 25:4-6). But the people of Judah had not listened. They seemed determined to provoke God to anger, though it had only resulted in harm to them (25:7).

2. Destruction by Babylon and Babylon's fate (25:8–14)

Because Judah had not obeyed Him, God was going to send Nebuchadnezzar at the head of a coalition of nations against her. The designation of Nebuchadnezzar as "my servant" (25:9; cf. 27:6; 43:10) has caused considerable discussion. How could God refer to the dedicated prophets as "his servants" (25:4) and also honor a pagan king with the same title? There is actually no conflict, for one may be a servant of God (i.e., used by Him for His purposes) willingly or unwittingly. It does not mean the Babylonian monarch worshiped the God of Israel.[4] God determined to use Nebuchadnezzar as His instrument of punishment against Judah and the surrounding nations. He was going to destroy them completely (25:9). The Hebrew word used here means to dedicate something to the Lord for complete destruction (cf. Deut. 20:1–18; Josh. 7; 1 Sam. 15).

The ordinary sounds of daily life were going to be silenced. Shouts of joy and gladness would not be heard in the streets, nor would the happy voices of bride and groom. The creaking sound of the millstone grinding grain would be stilled, for there would be no grain. There would be no oil for the lamps to illuminate the darkened houses (25:10). Desolation and servitude would continue for seventy years (25:11). At the end of seventy years the yoke would be lifted, and a righteous God would punish Babylon for her sins (25:12).

Two questions emerge from these verses. First, what period of time did the seventy years represent? They did, of course, represent the years of Judah's punishment (29:10; cf. Isa. 23:15–18). If calculated from 587, the fall of Jerusalem, the punishment should have ended in 517/16; but Judah was allowed to return by a decree of the Persian ruler Cyrus in 538 (cf. Ezra 1:1–4). The date 517/16 could, however, be understood as an appropriate time for marking the end of Judah's punishment, for the rebuilt temple was completed in 516 or 515 (cf. Zech. 1:12; Ezra 6:15).

The seventy years have also been calculated from 609 to 539, that is, from the death of Josiah and the beginning of Babylon's world domination to the fall of Babylon. The period has also been calculated from 605, when Babylon defeated Egypt, to 536, which is the probable year the first exiles returned after Cyrus signed his decree of 538. The

---

[4]Daniel 2:47; 3:29; 4:34–37 say that Nebuchadnezzar did acknowledge Israel's God, but he did not deny other gods. He worshiped many gods and had no difficulty in acknowledging one more.

period also has been interpreted symbolically to mean a long time or a normal life span, i.e., a whole generation is thought to have died in exile. Whatever the exact years were intended to be, seventy years represent a complete period of punishment, long enough to accomplish God's disciplining of His people.[5]

The other question involves God's use of a pagan nation to punish His own people (cf. Hab. 1); for wicked as His people were, they were not as bad as Babylon. The answer is not difficult to find. Though God did use Babylon to punish Judah, Babylon was still held accountable for its sins. It would be completely destroyed (25:12) and its people enslaved by others (25:14). Jeremiah's ability to predict a short seventy-years existence for a great world empire is testimony to the inspired nature of his prophecies. What other major empire in world history was of such short duration and yet made such an impact?[6]

3. The cup of God's wrath (25:15–29)

The account of the cup of the wine of wrath[7] has been interpreted either as a vision experienced by Jeremiah or as a symbolic act performed by him. If a symbolic act, did he really go to all the kings named and make them drink a cup of wine? It is unlikely he could have forced his way into the presence of Pharaoh or Nebuchadnezzar with such a demand. He would have been driven from their courts or perhaps killed. In recognition of the problem, some believe the entire experience was a vision. The latter interpretation would not detract from the message.

However, it is possible that Jeremiah symbolically forced the various rulers to drink the cup by approaching representatives of those nations who were in Jerusalem as envoys or merchants and demanding that they drink the wine. In support of this interpretation is the fact that

---

[5]Daniel's interpretation of the seventy years (Dan. 9) goes beyond the scope of this study.

[6]It may seem strange that Assyria, whose empire period lasted several centuries and inflicted such terror on neighboring nations, did not become the personification of evil in New Testament times rather than Babylon (see Rev. 14:8; 16:19; 17:5; 18:1–24). Babylon probably gained this dubious distinction because she was the one who destroyed the temple in Jerusalem. In the eyes of Jewish people no more horrible sin than that could be committed. It was the ultimate blasphemy (cf. Matt. 26:59–61).

[7]The origin of the cup of wrath is probably to be found in Numbers 5:11–31, the cup of the ordeal of jealousy (cf. Ps. 75:8; Isa. 51:17; Hab. 2:16; Lam. 4:21; Ezek. 23:31–34; Zech. 12:2; Mark 10:38; Rev. 14:10). When Jesus asked that the cup might pass from Him (Luke 22:42), He undoubtedly had reference to the cup as a symbol of God's wrath, as it is used in the Old Testament. God's wrath against sin fell on Him at the cross.

many representatives of kings of other nations were in Jerusalem (27:3).

Whether understood as a vision or as a symbolic act, the meaning is the same. The host-guest relationship is the key to its interpretation. God represented the host who would offer each guest a cup of wine. The nations named represented the guests. Jeremiah, the bearer of the message, represented the cupbearer who would offer the cup to each guest around the table. The wine itself represented God's judgment. "When they drink it, they will stagger and go mad because of the sword I will send among them" (25:16).

Most of the nations named in chapters 46–51 are found in these verses. One nation listed here that appears to be unknown is Sheshak (25:26; "Sheshach," NIV; cf. 51:41). Sheshak was a cryptic name for Babylon (cf. 51:1, where another cryptic name for Babylon is found).[8]

Those nations who might refuse to drink the wine would be ordered in the name of the Lord to drink it (25:28). In addition to its primary message of judgment of the nations, this act clearly teaches that the Lord is the universal God and judge of all nations. As Creator, it is His sovereign right to judge all peoples, even those who do not acknowledge Him as Lord. As a righteous God, He must punish sin wherever it is found.[9]

4. The coming of God in judgment on the nations (25:30–38)

The chapter closes with a vivid description of the coming invasion of the nations. In rapid succession the Lord is compared to a roaring lion, a treader of grapes (25:30) and a prosecutor, judge, and warrior (25:31). The invasion is compared to a great storm that is being stirred up (25:32). The resulting slaughter will be from one end of the earth to the other (25:33). It will be so great that there will be no proper burial or expressions of grief (25:33).

---

[8]"Sheshak" is formed by substituting the last letter of the Hebrew alphabet for the first, the next to the last for the second, etc., to arrive at the concealed name (sh–sh–k for b–b–l). This kind of code language is called an athbash. It would be like substituting z–y–x for a–b–c. Jeremiah was not, as some have suggested, afraid to mention Babylon out of fear of retaliation. He had already mentioned Babylon (25:8–14), and it will be mentioned again, even in the same verse with athbashes for Babylon (51:1, 41). The "athbash" was too simple for the Babylonians to be ignorant of its meaning. "Sheshak" could have been a byname, such as "the windy city" or "Lucifer," whose meaning was well-known but at the same time carried sinister overtones (cf. Isa. 21:11).

[9]The question of how God deals with those who never hear of Him or who follow another religion goes beyond the scope of this study but cannot be ignored. Whatever else could be contributed to a discussion of the problem, Christians affirm that God will deal justly with every individual. See Romans 1:20 for the implication that all are without excuse before God.

In a concluding word Jeremiah singled out the shepherds (i.e., leaders; cf. 23:1) for a special word of warning. They should begin to weep and wail and roll in the dust (a gesture of grief), for their time to be slaughtered has come (25:34). They will not be able to escape (25:35; cf. Amos 2:14), and their cries will be heard when God destroys the land ("their pasture," 25:36; cf. Zech. 11:3). God has already emerged like a lion from its lair to begin the carnage in Judah (25:38).

For Further Study

1. In a Bible dictionary or encyclopedia (see bibliography) read articles on: Nebuchadnezzar, Babylonia, Chaldea, heavenly council, signet ring, Sodom, and cup of wrath.

2. Make a study of the Old Testament concern for strangers, widows, and orphans.

3. What should be the characteristics of a good leader?

4. Could a person be a false prophet but sincerely believe that he is a spokesman for God?

5. Can God's justice be defended if He condemns people who have never had an opportunity to hear about Jesus Christ?

PART TWO: *Messages of Judgment and Hope*

Chapter 6

Jeremiah's Conflicts With the Leaders of Judah
(Jeremiah 26:1–29:32)

Jeremiah's messages brought him increasingly into conflict with the political and religious leaders of Judah. They justified their rejection of his warnings on "scriptural" grounds. They could cite the covenant that God made with Abraham (Gen. 12:1–3), giving them a land with no strings attached. They could cite the covenant that God made with Israel at Mount Sinai (Exod. 19:5–6), making them a chosen people. (At the same time they ignored the demands for obedience and faithfulness required by that covenant.) Finally, they could point to the covenant that God made with David (2 Sam. 7), promising that there would always be a king from his family seated on the throne of Israel.

Lulled by the confidence that God would always protect them, they rejected Jeremiah's warnings of destruction of their nation as blasphemous. If they had listened to Jeremiah, the history of Israel would have been quite different.[1]

A. The Temple Sermon (26:1–24)

Jeremiah understood what the leaders and people failed to see—that God's continued blessings were not dependent on superficial ritual, sacrifices, or a temple, but on their faithfulness to God. What more appropriate setting could be chosen than the temple itself for warning them that their confidence in ritual and a building were misplaced?

---

[1] The careful reader will notice that most of the narratives of chapters 26–45 are related in the third person, whereas chapters 1–25 are in the first person. This difference in style has led scholars to believe that 1–25 contains the narratives dictated by Jeremiah to Baruch (cf. 36:32), whereas 26–45 contains narratives about Jeremiah recorded by Baruch and others.

1. *Summary of the sermon* (26:1-6)

Early in the reign of Jehoiakim the Lord instructed Jeremiah to go stand in the court of the Lord's house and speak to the multitudes who came there to worship (26:2). Perhaps they would listen and turn from their evil ways so that God could "relent" (26:3; "repent," KJV). The Hebrew word does not imply that God made a mistake but rather it expresses His deep grief that resulted in a change of mind about His intended actions. In response to their repentance, He would relent concerning the disaster He was planning to bring on them because of their evil (26:3). God's condemnation was always conditional on the guilty one's repentance. If Judah would not listen, He would bring destruction on the temple and on Jerusalem as He had done at Shiloh (cf. 7:12-15 for comments).

Because the temple sermon here in chapter 26 sounds very much like the message of 7:1-15, many feel that both are accounts of the same event. If so, the emphasis of chapter 26 is on the response evoked by the message, while the emphasis of 7:1-15 is on the message itself, for it is given in greater detail. However, the explanation of the similarity may be that Jeremiah went to the temple on more than one occasion to deliver similar warnings.

2. *Jeremiah's arrest and trial* (26:7-19)

Priests, prophets ("false prophets," LXX), and a great crowd heard Jeremiah say that the temple could be destroyed. The Jews considered such words to be blasphemous, for the temple represented God's presence dwelling in their midst. They interpreted the prophet's words as a direct attack on the power and sovereignty of God. The message evoked such a violent reaction that the mob seized Jeremiah and was ready to kill him on the spot (26:8). They were probably also calling him a false prophet (Deut. 18:20).

The Hebrew word for "officials" (26:10), or leaders, could mean members of the royal household or court officials. They heard what had happened and gathered at the entrance of the New Gate of the temple. This gate, the location of which is uncertain, perhaps was the gate of 2 Kings 15:35, rebuilt by Jotham. There the leaders determined to try Jeremiah, amid the demands of the priests and prophets that he be put to death (26:11).

Jeremiah was allowed to speak. He insisted that the Lord had sent him to prophesy the words they had heard (26:12). He did not deny that he had pronounced disaster on Jerusalem, but he appealed to them to repent so that the Lord would change His mind and withhold the disaster He had pronounced against them (26:13). Jeremiah then cast himself on the mercy of his judges (26:14). At the same time he warned that if they did kill him, they would be bringing a curse on the city and all its inhabitants for spilling innocent blood (26:15; cf. Deut. 19:10; Jonah 1:14).

Jeremiah's defense convinced the leaders and the people that he did speak in the name of the Lord. They told the priests and prophets that Jeremiah should not be put to death (26:16). The term "elders" in verse 17 may be a technical term for local rulers; perhaps here it is used only of older men. A group of them arose to speak in Jeremiah's defense. They recalled that Micah had prophesied similar words a hundred years earlier during the reign of Hezekiah. Micah had warned that Jerusalem would be destroyed and the site of the temple would be covered with trees (26:18; cf. Mic. 3:12). This is the only occurrence in the Old Testament of a prophet being quoted by name citing another by name. They reminded the crowd that Hezekiah did not put Micah to death for warning of Jerusalem's destruction. Rather, he feared the Lord and entreated His favor (literally, "weakened the face," i.e., softened the countenance by stroking the face). On that occasion God relented and did not bring judgment (26:19).

3. Arrest and death of Uriah the prophet (26:20–23)

The seriousness of Jeremiah's situation for a few hours is revealed by a seemingly unrelated account of another prophet named Uriah ("Urijah," KJV). He also had preached against Jerusalem with words similar to those of Jeremiah (26:20). King Jehoiakim sought to put him to death, and so he fled to Egypt for sanctuary (26:21). However, Jehoiakim sent men to Egypt to bring him back. One of these men, Elnathan, later seemed to support Jeremiah (36:12, 25). As a vassal of Egypt, Jehoiakim would have no difficulty arranging extradition of a person accused of treason. Uriah was slain; his body was cast into the burial place of the common people and condemned criminals (26:23).

The episode reminds us that Jeremiah must have had supporters in high places, or else he would have suffered a similar fate at the hands of Jehoiakim. It also reminds us that Jeremiah was not the only prophet of the Lord in Judah.

4. *Jeremiah's release* (26:24)

The words of Jeremiah's defense had the effect of sufficiently placating the mob. Jeremiah was permitted to go free under Ahikam's protection. Ahikam was the father of Gedaliah, who later would become governor (26:24; cf. 39:14).

B. Struggle With the False Prophets (27:1–29:32)

Chapter 26 serves as an introduction to chapters 27–29. It tells how Jeremiah almost lost his life because he was accused of being a false prophet. Chapters 27–28 tell about a false prophet who challenged Jeremiah, and chapter 29 tells of some false prophets in Babylon.

1. *Jeremiah wears the symbolic yoke* (27:1–22)

In the next two chapters we find the longest recorded account of a symbolic act performed by Jeremiah. It involved a conflict with Hananiah, who claimed that God had spoken also to him.

a) *A warning to other nations to serve Babylon* (27:1–11)

In the beginning of the reign of Zedekiah (most Hebrew manuscripts say "Jehoiakim" but cf. 27:3, 12, 20; 28:1), the Lord instructed Jeremiah to place across his shoulders an ox's yoke (27:2). It consisted of wooden bars secured by leather cords about the neck. He was to send a message to kings of surrounding kingdoms by their envoys who were in Jerusalem (27:3; cf. comment at 51:59). He was to say that all those nations were going to be given over to Nebuchadnezzar, "my servant" (27:6; cf. 25:9). The nation that would not submit to the yoke of Babylon would be punished by the Lord through Nebuchadnezzar (27:8). Once again, God was making a claim of sovereignty over all nations (cf. discussion at 25:15–29).

Jeremiah warned them not to listen to their prophets, diviners, interpreters of dreams, mediums, or sorcerers who were assuring them that they would not serve Nebuchadnezzar (27:9). These men were speaking lies that would bring the nation to ruin (27:10). However, any nation that submitted to Babylon's yoke would be spared (27:11).

b) *A warning to Zedekiah* (27:12–15)

Jeremiah delivered a similar warning to King Zedekiah. The king should submit to the yoke of Babylon (27:12); he should not listen to the lies of prophets advising him not to submit to Babylon. Jeremiah warned that those false prophets were not from the Lord and were speaking lies in His name (27:14–15).

c) A warning to the priests and people (27:16–22)

Jeremiah made a similar appeal to the priests and the rest of the people not to listen to the false prophets. Those prophets were telling the people that the temple treasures captured by Nebuchadnezzar when Jehoiachin was carried to Babylon (27:20) would soon be returned from Babylon (27:16; cf. 1 Kings 7:15–50; Dan. 5:2; Ezra 1:7–11). If they were truly prophets, they should be praying that the remaining treasures would not be taken to Babylon (27:18). However, Jeremiah insisted that the rest of the treasures would be taken to Babylon and remain there until the Lord was ready to return them (27:22).

2. Conflict with Hananiah, the false prophet (28:1–17)

Jeremiah soon found his words being challenged by Hananiah, son of Azzur, otherwise unknown. He also claimed to have received a message from the Lord. He is called "the prophet Hananiah" six times in chapter 28 ("false prophet" in 28:1 of the LXX and elsewhere just "Hananiah").

a) Hananiah's prophecy and Jeremiah's response (28:1–9)

Hananiah confronted Jeremiah in the temple in the presence of the priests and a large number of people (28:1). He did not hesitate to preface his words with the authoritative introduction, "This is what the LORD Almighty, the God of Israel says" (28:2). Using Jeremiah's own symbolism, he predicted that the Lord "will break" the yoke of Nebuchadnezzar (28:2; "have broken," KJV, NASB; the verb is in the so-called prophetic perfect, found frequently in the Old Testament. The Hebrew perfect looks at action as completed and lends itself to a variety of English renderings. Although Nebuchadnezzar's yoke had not been broken, it was as good as done, since God said so).

Further, he said that all the articles from the temple that had been taken away would be returned within two years (28:3). Then, in open denial of an earlier prophecy of Jeremiah (22:24–27), Hananiah said Jehoiachin, who was still popularly considered as king of Judah although Zedekiah was on the throne, and all the other exiles would be returned to Judah (28:4). Hananiah's prophecies were not vague and general. He boldly set dates and gave specific names. He appeared willing to submit himself to the Deuteronomic test of true prophecy (Deut. 18:22).

Jeremiah recognized that Hananiah was challenging his authority as a prophet. However, rather than defend himself or precipitously call Hananiah a liar, he voiced a hope that Hananiah was speaking the truth: "Amen! May the LORD do so! May the LORD fulfill the words you have prophesied" (28:6). Jeremiah sincerely hoped that Hananiah was right. He also may have wondered whether the Lord had set him aside and was now speaking through someone else. He said that the only way to know whether a prophet had been sent from the Lord was to wait and see if his predictions were fulfilled (28:9; cf. Deut. 18:22).

b) *Hananiah's symbolic action* (28:10–11)

Emboldened by Jeremiah's meekness, Hananiah took the yoke from Jeremiah's neck and broke it in the presence of all the people (28:10). Then, after performing his own "symbolic act," he again announced that within two years the yoke of Nebuchadnezzar would be broken. Without a word and perhaps troubled by the thought that he was no longer the Lord's spokesman, Jeremiah walked away (28:11).

c) *Jeremiah's judgment on Hananiah* (28:12–17)

We are not told how much time elapsed after Jeremiah had been challenged by Hananiah. It is rather certain that Jeremiah spent time in prayer, seeking reassurance that what he had been preaching truly was God's message. He received that assurance, for the Lord told him to return to Hananiah and say, "You have broken a wooden yoke, but in its place you will get a yoke of iron" (28:13). God confirmed for Jeremiah that the nations would serve Nebuchadnezzar, wearing a yoke of iron (28:14).

The next time Jeremiah encountered Hananiah he had a word from the Lord for the false prophet. Using a subtle wordplay, he said, "The LORD has not sent you" (28:15), but "I am going to send you from the face of the earth" (28:16, literal translation). Hananiah was told he was going to die that same year because he had advised rebellion against the Lord. He had predicted deliverance in two years, but two months later he died (28:17; cf. 28:1).

3. *Letter to the exiles* (29:1–32)

This chapter contains a rare example of correspondence preserved in the Old Testament (cf. 2 Kings 19:14). It serves to remind that communication did continue back and forth between Jerusalem and Babylon during the period of exile.

a) A *warning against listening to false prophets* (29:1–23)

Jeremiah sent a letter from Jerusalem to the exiles who had been taken from Jerusalem in 597 along with King Jehoiachin, his mother, other officials, and craftsmen (29:1–2).

One of the letter carriers was Elasah, son of Shaphan (29:3). He probably was a brother of Ahikam (26:24) and a grandson of Josiah's scribe (2 Kings 22:8). The other letter carrier was Gemariah, son of Hilkiah (29:3), who was probably the high priest (2 Kings 22:4) rather than Jeremiah's father (1:1). Elasah and Gemariah were sent by Zedekiah to Nebuchadnezzar; the nature of their business is not stated. Perhaps they were sent to assure Nebuchadnezzar of Zedekiah's loyalty.

Jeremiah must have heard that some of the exiles did not believe they would remain for long in Babylon and were refusing to "unpack their bags." Therefore, in the letter he urged them to settle down there, build houses, plant gardens, marry, and increase in number (29:5–6). They should also seek the peace and prosperity of Babylon and should pray to the Lord for it (the only place in the Old Testament where a prophet gives a direct exhortation to pray for a pagan city). For if Babylon prospered, they would prosper (29:7; cf. Matt. 5:44). Jeremiah's suggestion that a devout Israelite could pray to God in pagan Babylon may have come as a surprise to the exiles, who probably shared a popular belief that the gods were limited geographically.

Jeremiah warned that they should not listen to the false prophets and diviners, who apparently were telling them they would soon return home (29:8–9). Jeremiah's letter makes clear that for the most part the exiles were not subjected to harsh imprisonment and rigorous servitude.

The return would not be soon, but they would return after seventy years had been completed for Babylon (29:10; cf. discussion at 25:11–12). The seventy years here refer to the duration of the Babylonian empire; it fell to the Persians in 539 B.C.

God assured the exiles that He had not forgotten them. He had plans for them that would prosper them and not hurt them (29:11). What God was doing was for their well-being (cf. Rom. 8:28). He encouraged them to pray to Him, for He would listen to them. The word "heart" in 29:13 refers to the seat of the intellect, not the emotions. If they would seek Him and search for Him with all their heart, they would find Him; and He would restore them to their land (29:13–14).

Jeremiah warned the exiles against listening to false prophets. He told them that those remaining in Judah would be ravaged by sword, famine, and plague so that they would become like rotten (literally, "split open") figs that could not be eaten (29:17; cf. 24:1–10). They would become abhorrent and a reproach to all nations because they had not listened to the Lord's words sent by His servants the prophets (29:18–19; cf. 19:8).

The exiles could profit from the warning by listening to the word of the Lord. Jeremiah warned them to learn a lesson from Ahab and Zedekiah, otherwise unknown, who at that moment were prophesying falsely in the Lord's name (29:21) and were committing adultery (29:23). God was going to deliver them to Nebuchadnezzar, who would have them burned to death in public. Hananiah already had died for prophesying falsely (28:15–17). Now two more were condemned.

The memory of the punishment of these two false prophets inspired the exiles later to compose a proverbial-like curse to be used for one's enemies: "The LORD treat you like Zedekiah and Ahab, whom the king of Babylon burned in the fire" (29:22).

b) A message to Shemaiah (29:24–32)

Jeremiah addressed the remainder of his letter to one of the exiles named Shemaiah of Nehelem (a family name or an unknown town). Shemaiah had sent letters to the people in Jerusalem, to Zephaniah the priest (cf. 21:1), and to the other priests (29:25). He reminded Zephaniah that the Lord had made him priest instead of Jehoiada to be in charge of the temple (29:26; cf. 52:24). He told Zephaniah that it was his responsibility to put any madman into stocks and neck-irons who pretended to be a prophet (29:26; cf. 20:1–2). He then took the priest to task for being negligent in his duty to rebuke Jeremiah (29:27). Shemaiah concluded that Jeremiah was a false prophet and worthy of the stocks because he was advising the exiles to build houses, settle down, and plant gardens because the exile was going to be long (29:28).

When Zephaniah received Shemaiah's letter, he read it to Jeremiah (29:29), perhaps as a friend or as a warning. Jeremiah replied to Shemaiah's letter by accusing him of being a false prophet (29:31). He told Shemaiah that the Lord was going to punish him and his descendants. He would not live to see the end of the exile or have descendants because his words encouraged rebellion against the Lord (29:32).

For Further Study

1. In a Bible dictionary or encyclopedia (see bibliography) read articles on: repentance, elder, and false prophet.

2. What are some characteristics of a false prophet whereby he could be distinguished from a true prophet?

3. What are some lessons that can be learned from the death of Hananiah?

4. Would you have called Jeremiah a traitor if you had lived in 597 B.C., and heard him appeal to the people to submit to the yoke of Babylon?

5. What did God hope to accomplish on behalf of His people through the Babylonian exile?

Chapter 7

Some Messages of Hope
(Jeremiah 30:1–33:26)

The dominant theme of the Book of Jeremiah up to this point has been judgment on Judah for her sins. However, Jeremiah did not foresee only calamity and destruction for Judah. He understood that purging was necessary if God were to bring His people into a new and lasting relationship with Himself. He believed that God still had future plans for His people. It was, therefore, not inconsistent for him to preach messages both of judgment and of hope. In chapters 30–33 are grouped some of Jeremiah's most eloquent assurances of hope for the future.[1] These chapters are sometimes called "The Book of Comfort" or "The Book of Consolation" because of their optimism about the future.

A. Promise of a New Covenant and a Restored Nation (30:1–31:40)

Because of her disobedience Israel failed to enjoy the covenant blessings promised her. Yet God still desired to bless His people. If blessing could not be achieved through a covenant conditioned on obedience, then He would make another covenant with His people. Jeremiah was not the only prophet to speak about another covenant, but he is the only one in the Old Testament who called it a "new covenant" (31:31). The full import of his words can be understood only against the background of the New Testament, which more accurately should be called the New Covenant.

---

[1]Critics are divided about the authorship of these four chapters. Some say Jeremiah wrote none of these words. Others say he wrote a core. There is no agreement among them concerning the words they would accept as genuine Jeremianic. When critics are in such hopeless disagreement, it suggests that the literary and historical evidence is not sufficient to discard Jeremianic authorship.

1. Introduction (30:1-3)

The Lord instructed Jeremiah to write down the words He had spoken to him (30:2). The command does not refer to the occasion when Jeremiah dictated his messages to Baruch (36:32). It is intended to serve as an introduction to the messages of hope for the future that now appear in the book. The Lord wanted His people to know that "days are coming . . . when I will bring my people Israel and Judah back from captivity and restore them to the land I gave their forefathers" (30:3). The promises were for Israel and Judah.

2. Promise of deliverance for Jacob (30:4-11)

God looked beyond Jeremiah's time to see a time of fear and terror when strong men would be doubled up in pain like a woman in labor and faces would be pale from dread (30:6). The cause of their fear was "a time of trouble for Jacob" (30:7), a reference here to all Israel; but the nation would be saved out of it. In that day the Lord would break their yoke of servitude to other peoples (30:8). Then they would serve "the LORD their God and David their king, whom I will raise up for them" (30:9). The promise of a restored David was never understood as a literal resurrection of King David, but as an ideal king of his family.

One interpretation of these remarkable words insists that they speak only of a historical return from the Babylonian exile. This did take place; however, no Davidic king regained the throne. Thus the meaning of the prophecy cannot be exhausted in the events that immediately followed the return to Judah after 538 B.C.

The Old Testament frequently uses such phrases as "in that day" (Isa. 2:20; cf. Zeph. 2:15), "in the future" (Dan. 10:14), "days are coming" (Jer. 49:2), or "the day of the LORD" (Amos 5:18-20; cf. Joel 2:31). A careful study of all the passages that contain such phrases will eliminate the supposition that they refer only to events that have already occurred historically.[2]

---

[2]Eschatologically, the Day of the Lord in the Old Testament is the time in history when God will vindicate Himself. Accompanied by cosmic phenomena (Joel 2:31), it will be universal (Obad. 15) and a time of judgment of God's enemies and deliverance of the faithful (Isa. 13:6; Mal. 4:1-3). A better world will emerge, characterized by a transformation of nature (Amos 9:13; Zech. 14:6-7), of relations between man and his environment (Isa. 11:6-8), and of human relations (Mic. 4:3). Zion will be exalted (Zech. 14:16). The Old Testament always speaks of the Day of the Lord as near at hand (Isa. 13:6), much as the New Testament speaks of the Second Coming. The New Testament takes up the theme of the Day of the Lord and adds immeasurably to its content with its final and climactic fulfillment described in the Book of Revelation.

Jeremiah, as did other prophets, foresaw a Davidic king as a key to the Day of the Lord. Though Jeremiah probably did not understand the full implications of his own words, the New Testament is careful to show that Jesus Christ is of the family of David and, as the eternal Son of God, is the fulfillment of the promises of a Davidic king that were first made to David (2 Sam. 7). During Jesus' lifetime the Jewish people as a nation did not accept Him as their long-awaited King, and that is still the case today. However, some Jews have individually accepted Christ as the fulfillment of the Old Testament messianic promises.

The Lord comforted Jacob His servant by exhorting him not to be afraid (30:10; cf. Isa. 44:1-2). God was going to deliver His people from their captivity and once again give them peace and security. He would destroy the nations that had scattered them, and He would discipline His people with justice. However, He assured them that He would not destroy them completely (30:10-11; cf. 46:27-28). The promise of a remnant is a recurring theme throughout the Old Testament (cf. comment at 4:27).

3. *Promise of healing of a terrible wound* (30:12-17)

It must have appeared to Judah that her wound was incurable and her injury beyond healing with no one to help. Jeremiah compared her to a soldier mortally wounded in battle. All her political allies ("lovers," KJV, NASB) had forgotten her, and even God had wounded her like an enemy because of her many sins (30:14).

What kind of comfort could words like these have brought to Judah? In verses 16-17 we find the answer. All those who had mistreated Judah would themselves be punished; they were going to be devoured and plundered (30:16; cf. Matt. 7:2). A gracious God promised to restore the health of Zion (a name for Jerusalem in the Old Testament, from a word that probably means "parched ground") and to heal her wounds (30:17). The verses contain a very moving reminder that God cares for the outcasts and is willing to forgive those who sin against Him. He cares for those for whom no one else cares (30:17).

4. *Promise of restoration of Jacob's fortunes* (30:18-22)

The Lord promised to restore the "fortunes" (literally, "the captivity") of Jacob's tents (30:18). He promised that Jerusalem would be rebuilt on her "ruins" (Hebrew, *tel*, from a word, "to heap up"). The king's palace would stand in its proper place once again. There would be thanksgiving, rejoicing, restoration of respect for Israel, and the reestablishment of her former stability (30:19–20).

Again the promise of a restored ruler was given (30:21; cf. 23:5–6; 33:14–16), but in language that Christians see as fulfilled in Jesus Christ. Their "leader" ("prince," JB; KJV translates incorrectly as a plural, "nobles") would be one of them. The words suggest that the future king was going to be an Israelite from a lowly family (cf. Matt. 8:20; Luke 2:7).

The restored ruler would also have the qualities of a priest; for the words, "I will bring him near and he will come close to me" (30:21), speak of the priest who alone was permitted to approach the Lord. For a priest to enter the divine presence uninvited was to risk death (cf. Exod. 28:34–35). It is evident that 30:21 is included among the messianic utterances of Jeremiah, though its language is not so specific as other messianic passages.

The result of God's restored favor—the return of the people, the rebuilding of the cities, and a new ruler—will be a restored covenant relationship that is expressed in covenant language: "You will be my people, and I will be your God" (30:22).

5. *Promise of punishment of the wicked* (30:23–31:1)

The chapter closes with another vivid threat of punishment of the wicked. God's wrath is described as a storm, a driving wind swirling down on the heads of the wicked (30:23). His anger will not be abated until He has fully accomplished the purposes of His heart (30:24). The oracle concludes with a cryptic statement, "In days to come you will understand this" ("In the latter days . . ." KJV, RSV, NASB).

6. *Promise of return of the exiles (31:2–14)*

Jeremiah spoke of finding grace "in the desert" (31:2; cf. 2:2–8). The statement has been interpreted as a reference to the Exodus from Egypt or as the return from exile and dispersion among the nations. God reminded His people that He had loved them with an everlasting love (31:3). The prodigal was still His child. Because of that love they could be sure that He would rebuild the nation (31:4). Though the prophets had frequently described Israel as a harlot because of her faithlessness (e.g., Hos. 4:15; Ezek. 23:3), God could look beyond her present condition and see her in the purity of an ideal, restored relationship. Therefore, He could speak of her as the "Virgin Israel" (31:4; cf. 14:17; 18:13; 31:21; 46:11; Amos 5:2).

Amid peace and security, Israel would again make music, dance joyfully (31:4), plant her vineyards on the hills of Samaria, and "enjoy their fruit" (31:5; literally, "profane them," i.e., put the fruit to common use after the period had elapsed when it was considered holy; cf. Lev. 19:23–25; Deut. 20:6). The time was coming when the watchmen on the hills of Ephraim, upon seeing the new moon in the sky, would call out to the people that it was time to go to Zion (i.e., Jerusalem; cf. 30:17) to worship the Lord (31:6). The rift between God and His people would come to an end. The divided worship that began after the death of Solomon would be forgotten (cf. 1 Kings 12:25–33), and all the tribes would come to Jerusalem to worship.

The remnant of Israel (cf. 4:27) was going to be brought back from the ends of the earth singing and giving praise ("hallelujah" comes from this word; 31:7–8). The great throng would come with weeping to the refreshing streams of water and not stumble (31:9). God would take care of them because He was their father and Ephraim was His "firstborn son" (31:9). In a chronological sense Reuben was Jacob's eldest son (Gen. 29:32); however, the term "firstborn" was applied by God to Ephraim due to that tribe's recognized leadership among the other tribes during the time of the northern kingdom. The name Ephraim was thus a synonym for the whole northern kingdom of Israel.

God was not only the father of His people but was also the shepherd who would keep His flock Israel (31:10). The Lord promised to ransom Jacob and redeem[3] him from those who had subjugated him (31:11). Jeremiah described a time of joy, with abundance of food and herds with all sorrow of the past removed for both priest and people (31:12–14).

7. *Rachel's weeping and return of her children* (31:15–22)

Jeremiah compared the scattering of Israel to Rachel raising her head from the grave in Ramah to weep on seeing the land depopulated

---

[3]"Ransom" is from a Hebrew word that means "to loose," thus to set free by paying a price. It was first used in commercial transactions, suggesting payment to deliver from physical danger. "Redeem" is a word that means "to buy back." It refers to the process by which something alienated was recovered for the original owner. It was first used to describe obligations to the members of one's family, such as recovering property that had been sold (Lev. 25:25), marrying a deceased brother's widow who was childless (Deut. 25:5–10), avenging the murder of a near kinsman (Num. 35:19), or buying a kinsman out of slavery (Lev. 25:47–48). Both words were used in everyday life before they were given the theological significance associated with God's redemption.

of her descendants (31:15). Rachel died in childbirth on the way to Bethlehem (Gen. 35:19; cf. 48:7) and was buried at Zelzah on the border of Benjamin (1 Sam. 10:2). The weeping refers to the grief for the northern tribes who were destroyed as a nation by the Assyrians in 722 B.C., and taken into exile. In these verses God is depicted as consoling Rachel with the promise of restoration of her children from exile (31:16–17; cf. Matt. 2:17–18 for a New Testament fulfillment of these words).

Ephraim's rebellion was compared to an unruly calf that required disciplining (31:18). God wanted to hear His people say, "Restore me, and I will return, . . . After I strayed, I repented" (31:18–19). His anger with Ephraim was overshadowed by His love for him (31:20; cf. Hos. 11:8–9).

God's grief concerning His rebellious people is expressed in 31:20 as only parents of wayward children can understand. He had spoken against what they were doing; yet they were His dear children in whom He delighted and whom He remembered. He yearned for a restored relationship, and He would have compassion on them (31:20; "my bowels are troubled," KJV; cf. 4:19).

God appealed to His wayward people to return to Him. The traveler in going forth set up road markers so that when he returned he would not lose his way; likewise, Israel was encouraged to return to God by the same way she had gone away (31:21).[4]

In perhaps the most cryptic verse in the Book of Jeremiah, the Lord appealed to His faithless daughter to return, for "The LORD will create a new thing on earth—a woman will surround a man" (31:22). The verse has been interpreted to refer to a woman wooing a man (i.e.,

---

[4]The many passages in Jeremiah and the rest of the Old Testament that speak of a return of Israel to the land have been responsible for three principal interpretations of this promise. One view is that all the promises were fulfilled historically when Israel returned to her land after the Babylonian exile ended. A second view is that these passages contain promises that go beyond what actually took place, and therefore there is a yet future return of Israel to her land. The present restoration of the state of Israel is seen by many as the beginning of the fulfillment of these promises. However, many conservative scholars notice that the promises of return are for an Israel that has already repented and returned to God (Deut. 30:1–4); hence the return of recent years is not the ultimate biblical fulfillment. Still others interpret the fulfillment as spiritual rather than political and geographical in nature (Rom. 9:8).

The fact that the Jewish people continue to exist when, like other ancient peoples, they should have lost their identity and been assimilated among other peoples, indicates that God is not through with His people (cf. Rom. 11). It is better to leave the details of what God plans to do with the Jews in His hands rather than to work out detailed chronological charts and timetables, as many well-intentioned Christians have done.

Israel will seek God), a woman protecting a man (i.e., Israel will once again be strong), and as a woman having a son (i.e., messianically, the conception of Jesus). Whatever the exact meaning intended, the verse does say that something unusual is going to happen. The "new thing" the Lord will create is somehow linked to the restoration of Israel.

8. *Promise of future blessing* (31:23-28)

The time will come when the people of Judah have returned to their land and will call on God to bless the temple, here called a "righteous dwelling" and a "sacred mountain" (31:23). In that time the Lord will "refresh the weary and satisfy the faint" (31:25).

It appears that God had been speaking to Jeremiah through a dream, for at this juncture Jeremiah awoke (31:26). The interruption in the text is unusual.

The promises of future restoration then continue. Using the figure of a farmer planting seed, the Lord said that the time was coming when He would "plant," or repopulate, Israel and Judah with men and animals (31:27). Furthermore, even as He had uprooted and torn down, so He was going to build and plant them again (31:28; cf. 1:10).

9. *Promise of individual retribution* (31:29-30)

The people of Judah were unwilling to accept the fact that their own sins were bringing God's punishment on them. They shifted the blame by insisting that previous generations had committed sins for which they were being punished. Supported by their interpretation of the second commandment (Exod. 20:5), a popular proverb was current among them: "The fathers have eaten sour grapes, and the children's teeth are set on edge" (31:29). It would be strange to bite into a green persimmon and hear a person standing nearby complain that his teeth felt the acid of the sour fruit. Yet in effect Judah was saying that this transfer was occurring. The people were unwilling to accept responsibility for their sins. So Jeremiah made it very clear that each person was held accountable for his sins, not for the sins of someone else: "Everyone will die for his own sin" (31:30; cf. Ezek. 18:2-4).

10. *Promise of a new covenant* (31:31-34)

The importance of the covenant in God's relationship with Israel cannot be overestimated. It frequently has been called the central theme of the Bible, the "glue that holds it together." God made covenants with Noah (Gen. 9:8–17), Abraham (Gen. 12:1–3), Israel (Exod. 19), David (2 Sam. 7), and others in the Old Testament.

The covenant made at Mount Sinai was conditioned on obedience, but Israel had a history of disobedience (31:32). Yet God still wanted to maintain a relationship with her. Therefore, He announced through Jeremiah that He was going to make a "new covenant" with Israel and Judah (31:31; cf. 1 Cor. 11:25). This is the only time in the Old Testament that the phrase "new covenant" is found, though the idea is expressed in different ways elsewhere. Of all Jeremiah's messages, the announcement of the new covenant is undoubtedly the most important of all his teachings.

Jeremiah described five significant characteristics of the new covenant. First, God was going to take the initiative in establishing the covenant. Observe the frequent use of "I," "me," and "my" in 31:31–34. The Bible is the story of man's flight from God in the opening chapters of Genesis and God's pursuit of man to the last pages of Revelation to restore that broken fellowship.

The second characteristic of the new covenant is that it will be inward. It will be in the mind and written on the heart, not on tablets of stone. Under the new covenant people will obey God because they want to, not because they feel obligated or threatened ("Christ's love compels us," 2 Cor. 5:14).

A third characteristic of the new covenant is that it will be established on an individual basis. Each one will come to know God through individual decision. There will be no need of religious instruction, for each one will have the right of access to God.

Another characteristic of the new covenant is its universality. All will know Him, from the least to the greatest. The passage does not imply universal salvation but a time of separation by judgment (cf. Matt. 25:31–33). Only those who have accepted Jesus Christ as Savior will remain to enjoy the new covenant relationship (cf. Rev. 20–22).

A final characteristic of the new covenant is that it will be based on God's forgiveness (31:34). Christians are unanimous in their belief that the new covenant of which Jeremiah spoke was established by Jesus Christ through His death and resurrection.

It should be noted that Jeremiah's promise of a new covenant was made specifically to Israel and Judah (31:31). Salvation for the Jew will come through the new covenant, not through renewal of the Mosaic covenant. The New Testament says that Jesus first came to the Jewish people (John 1:11), and only after they rejected Him was the gospel taken to the Gentiles (Acts 10:15, 34–35; 13:46; 15:7–9).

11. *Promise of eternal duration of the nation* (31:35–37)

In order to emphasize the fact that His love for Israel was unchangeable and eternal, God said there was as much chance of His casting away Israel as there was of the fixed order of the sun and moon or the ocean waves disappearing (31:35–36). It was as unlikely that Israel would be rejected as that someone would be able to measure the total extent of the universe and search out all the secrets of the foundations of the earth (31:37). The preservation of the Jewish people to the present time is an affirmation of this promise.

12. *Promise that Jerusalem will be rebuilt* (31:38–40)

Though Jeremiah had earlier warned that Jerusalem would be destroyed (26:6), now the Lord promised that it would be rebuilt. (Consult a Bible encyclopedia for discussion of the various places named in 31:38–40.) The entire area would be holy to the Lord and would never be destroyed again (cf. Rev. 21:2).

B. Jeremiah's Purchase of a Field in Anathoth (32:1–44)

1. *Jeremiah's imprisonment during the siege of Jerusalem* (32:1–5)

Jeremiah's warnings about the destruction of Jerusalem were now being fulfilled. It was the tenth year of Zedekiah's reign, 588 B.C., and Jerusalem was already under siege by Nebuchadnezzar's army (32:1–2). Jeremiah had been shut up in the courtyard of the guard, which was not a dungeon for common criminals but a place for privileged prisoners. He had been confined because of his "doomsday" messages concerning Jerusalem and the king himself that were demoralizing Jerusalem's will to resist (32:3–5; cf. chapter 37 for further events of Jeremiah's imprisonment). The leaders did not want the people to hear Jeremiah's call for surrender to the enemy.

2. *Jeremiah's purchase of a field* (32:6–15)

The Lord informed Jeremiah that his cousin Hanamel was coming to ask him to buy his field at Anathoth (32:7). As nearest relative, it was Jeremiah's duty under the law to redeem family land. Under the law every effort was made to keep property from being sold outside the family (Lev. 25:25–28; cf. Ruth 4:1–12; 1 Kings 21:3). Hanamel's financial straits may have forced him to sell the land, or he may have been one of the men of Anathoth who plotted against Jeremiah (11:21; 18:18). Perhaps they were testing Jeremiah's sincerity about his messages of hope for the future.

The transaction probably took place during a lull in the siege (cf. 37:11–12), else Hanamel could not have entered Jerusalem. When the cousin arrived, Jeremiah purchased the field and weighed out the purchase price, seventeen shekels of silver (32:9; the exact value is unknown, but one shekel was about 2/5 oz.).

Following practices then current, Jeremiah signed and sealed the deed before witnesses and weighed out the silver (32:10). He gave the deed to Baruch (32:12; the first mention of Jeremiah's scribe) and instructed him to take the two copies of the deed, one sealed and the other opened for easy reference, and to place them in a clay jar for safekeeping and for protection against unauthorized alterations (32:14). Archaeologists have verified that legal documents, whether clay or papyrus, were duplicated just as Jeremiah described.

The purchase of the field at Anathoth served as another of Jeremiah's symbolic acts. The purpose of this transaction was to demonstrate confidence that houses, fields, and vineyards would once again be bought and sold in Judah (32:15), though such a possibility seemed remote with Babylon's armies outside Jerusalem's walls. The message gave hope in the midst of a hopeless situation that life would return to normal in Judah.

3. *Jeremiah's prayer for understanding* (32:16–25)

It took much faith on Jeremiah's part to pay for a piece of property when real estate values were at an all-time low. It could be called a test of "Put your money where your mouth is." Titles to all property would be made worthless by Babylon's conquest, whereas the silver could have been used to purchase food for survival. Jeremiah acted in faith, however, and affirmed that nothing was too difficult for God (32:17), i.e., even the deliverance of Judah from her present distress. He acknowledged God's love (32:18), power, and justice (32:19). He recalled the plagues in Egypt (32:20), the Exodus, and the conquest of the Promised Land as evidences of God's past mighty acts on behalf of His people (32:21–22).

He further acknowledged that because Israel had been disobedient, the Lord had brought the present calamity on the city (32:23).

However, having acknowledged God's greatness and power, Jeremiah seemed amazed that God had asked him to purchase the field in Anathoth (32:25). Jeremiah's faith was strained to the limit to believe that the Babylonian calamity could be reversed, and he needed reassurance.

4. *God's answer to the prayer* (32:26–44)

The Lord responded to Jeremiah's prayer by assuring him that nothing was too difficult for the "God of all mankind" (32:27; cf. 32:17). He told Jeremiah that His power was revealed in two ways: (1) through His judgment on Jerusalem and its imminent destruction (32:28–36); and (2) by the subsequent restoration of His people from all the lands where He was scattering them (32:37). He would bring them back, and they would be His people and He their God (32:38). He would unify them in singleness of heart and action (32:39). He would make an everlasting covenant with them (32:40; cf. 31:31–34; Isa. 55:3; Ezek. 16:60), and put fear[5] of Him in their hearts.

In a final response to Jeremiah's prayer, God told him that though the land was a desolation and given over to the Babylonians, life would return to normal. Property would again be bought and sold. Deeds would be signed, sealed, and deposited for safekeeping, as symbolized by Jeremiah's purchase of property from a kinsman (32:43–44).

C. Promises of Restoration (33:1–26)

1. *Restoration of Jerusalem* (33:1–9)

The Lord spoke a second time to Jeremiah while he was still confined in the courtyard of the guard (33:1; cf. 32:2). Perhaps Jeremiah needed reassurance for himself or reassurance concerning the future of Judah. God invited him, "Call to me and I will answer you and tell you great and unsearchable things you do not know" (33:3). The invitation suggests that divine revelation becomes reality when it is sought (cf. Matt. 7:7). Jerusalem was under siege, and the people had resorted to desperate measures to save themselves. Royal dwellings were torn down, and their rubble was heaped up to raise barricades

---

[5]The fear of God in the Old Testament can mean dread or terror (Deut. 1:29; 2 Chron. 17:10); but it can also mean respect (Ps. 19:9), reverence (2 Kings 17:7; Ps. 2:11), love (Deut. 10:12, 20), knowledge (Prov. 1:29), service (Deut. 6:13), or obedience (Gen. 20:11; 2 Kings 4:1; Prov. 1:7). In 32:40 the "fear" includes elements of respect, service, and obedience; for it is fear written in the heart (cf. 31:33).

and reinforce the walls and defenses against the siege ramps the Babylonians were building (33:4; cf. Isa. 22:9–10).

God said He had hidden His face from Jerusalem because of its wickedness, i.e., He would show no compassion for their pleas (33:5). Yet He was going to heal the city and the people and let them enjoy peace and security (33:6; cf. 30:17). He was going to pardon all their iniquities (33:8).[6] Jerusalem would then bring renown, joy, praise, and honor to God before all the nations (33:9). It seems that the closer the city came to destruction, the greater the intensity of Jeremiah's emphasis on hope for the future.

2. *Restoration of joy* (33:10–11)

The city that was now desolate would again ring with voices of joy and of people bringing their thank offerings to the temple (33:10–11; cf. 25:10).

3. *Restoration of the flocks* (33:12–13)

In the now desolate land, flocks would once again "pass under the hand of the one who counts them" (33:13). The phrase describes the shepherd who counts his sheep each evening as they come into the fold to be sure that none is missing (cf. 31:24).

4. *Restoration of the Davidic kingdom and the Levitical priesthood* (33:14–26)

Again Jeremiah announced the coming of a righteous Branch of David under whose leadership Judah would be saved and Jerusalem would dwell in safety (33:15–16; cf. 23:5–6). The city would be known as "The LORD Our Righteousness" (cf. comment on 23:6). There would always be a Davidic king to rule Israel (33:17), and there would always be Levitical priests to present sacrifices to the Lord (33:18).

In applying the hermeneutical rule that prophecy as well as other portions of Scripture should be interpreted literally, when possible, or in its normal meaning, many Bible scholars understand verse 18 to mean that the Old Testament sacrificial system will be literally restored

---

[6]This verse contains the three major words for sin in the Old Testament (cf. Ps. 51:1–2). Each word reveals a different facet of the Hebrew understanding of the true nature of sin. "Iniquity" is from a word that means "twisted" or "bent," hence distorted or perverted. "Sin" is from a word that means "to miss the mark," as an archer missing a target, or "miss the way," as one taking a wrong road. "Transgression" is from a word that means "to rebel."

at some future time. Others interpret the restored sacrificial system as a memorial ritual during the millennium. Other Bible scholars contend that if the restoration of the Davidic king promised in the preceding verse is considered to be fulfilled in Christ, then it is reasonable to interpret the Levitical priest as being fulfilled by Christ in His priestly role (Heb. 7:23–28; cf. Zech. 6:13). Ultimately, the view that one adopts depends on his hermeneutics.

Again Jeremiah pointed to the unchangeable cycle of day and night as evidence that God's covenant with David could never be broken (33:20–21; cf. 31:35–37; Gen. 8:22). It was as dependable as day and night! The descendants of David and the Levites will be as numerous as the stars in the heavens and the sands of the sea (33:22; cf. Gen. 22:17).

God usually referred to Israel as "my people," but the expression, "these people," in verse 24 may be a subtle way of communicating estrangement from God. The critics, evidently Jews in despair, were saying that God had rejected both Israel and Judah ("the two families," KJV). However, the lack of faith of some did not nullify God's covenant. There was as much chance of God's covenant with His people being rejected as there was for the endless cycle of day and night to be broken (33:25–26).

For Further Study

1. In a Bible dictionary or encyclopedia (see bibliography) read articles on: Rachel's tomb, covenant, remnant, and fear of God.

2. What are some positive contributions to our lives through the experience of personal suffering?

3. Why was it so difficult for Judah to learn a lesson from Israel's downfall?

4. Do *you* really believe that nothing is too difficult for God?

Chapter 8

Jeremiah's Encounters With Disobedience and Obedience
(Jeremiah 34:1–36:32)

The closer Jerusalem approached destruction, the more intense became Jeremiah's efforts to warn the city. He offered only one solution for the impending tragedy; it was to surrender to the enemy. His advice would require obedience and absolute confidence in the commands of God. Judah had not been an obedient people for centuries; so the prophet had little reason to hope for a change now. When the people freed their slaves during the siege, he may have briefly entertained the hope that they were changing. But as soon as they thought the siege was lifted and the danger past, they canceled their slaves' freedom (34:11; 37:5, 11). Jeremiah had to look outside the family of Judah to find obedience, and he found it among the Recabites.

A. A Warning to King Zedekiah (34:1–7)

During the height of Nebuchadnezzar's siege of Jerusalem, the Lord sent Jeremiah to King Zedekiah with another warning (34:1). He told him the city was going to capitulate and be burned with fire and Zedekiah would be taken prisoner. He would see Nebuchadnezzar "face to face" (34:3; literally, "his mouth with your mouth"). However, He did promise that the king would die peacefully, i.e., a nonviolent death, and that his death would be observed by ceremonial honor (34:5; cf. 2 Chron. 16:14; 21:19).

Jeremiah delivered the warning to the king when only Jerusalem, Lachish, and Azekah remained untaken of the fortified cities of Judah (34:7). Archaeologists have uncovered broken bits of pottery at Lachish from the period of Jerusalem's siege. On one of them was inscribed a message from an officer of a military outpost to the garrison commander at Lachish saying he was watching for signals from Lachish (less than thirty miles southwest of Jerusalem) and could not see the signal fires of Azekah (fifteen miles southwest of Jerusalem). He was probably writing after Azekah had fallen to the Babylonians.

B. The Broken Pledge to Free the Slaves (34:8–22)

According to the Mosaic law, Hebrew slaves were to be released at the end of six years (Exod. 21:2–11; Lev. 25:39–46; Deut. 15:1, 12–18). Servitude could not extend for an indefinite period. However, even as Judah had disregarded other laws for years, it is not surprising that slave owners did not release their slaves at the end of the prescribed time, as it would have been an economic loss to them.

However, during the siege of Jerusalem, they did release their slaves. Their motives were probably mixed. Some masters released their slaves as a practical consideration, as it had become an economic burden to feed and take care of them. Others felt that if the slaves were freed, they would more likely help defend the city. Some piously believed that if the slaves were freed, God would take note of their obedience and save Jerusalem. Perhaps a few were motivated by genuine repentance.

For most, however, the release was a pious fraud, a kind of "foxhole religion" that makes sweeping vows to God in time of crisis but quickly forgets the vows when the crisis is past.

We are not told why they had a change of heart and revoked their slaves' release. However, it probably occurred when the siege was lifted temporarily (cf. 34:21; 37:5). The slaveholders mistakenly thought the Babylonians would not return and regretted their rash action of freeing the slaves (34:11).

The Lord had a message for such people. He instructed Jeremiah to remind them they had once been slaves in Egypt (34:13) and that the law specifically required the release of Hebrew slaves at the end of seven years.[1] Though their forefathers had ignored the law of liberation (34:14), the once-enslaved people should have been compassionate toward other slaves. God was pleased with the release of the slaves in besieged Jerusalem (34:15). Now, however, He accused the slave own-

---

[1]The law said they were to be freed after six years (Exod. 21:2), but 34:14 says "seven" ("six," LXX). There is no contradiction, however. The seventh year was probably considered a sabbatic year (cf. Exod. 23:10–11), during which the slave did not work, with his legal freedom granted at the end of the seventh year (cf. Deut. 15:1, 12).

ers of profaning (from a word "to pierce") His name by taking back their slaves (34:16).

God takes vows seriously regardless of the circumstances under which they are made (Ps. 76:11; Eccl. 5:4–6). Therefore, He was angry with the slave owners in Jerusalem. In an ironical wordplay, He said that because they did not proclaim freedom for their fellow country-men, He was going to proclaim freedom for the slave owners—but a different kind of freedom. He was going to free them over to the sword, plague, and famine (34:17).

The officials, priests, and others had hypocritically affirmed the covenant by walking between the cut up pieces of a calf (an ancient covenant ratification ceremony that implied a similar fate for either party breaking the covenant; 34:18–19; cf. Gen. 15:17). Because of their disobedience, God said He would treat them like the calf which had been cut in pieces. They were going to be handed over to their enemies. Their dead bodies would serve as food for the birds and wild animals (34:20; cf. 7:33), a fate considered horrible because proper burial would be denied to the corpses. Zedekiah and his officials would also be turned over to the Babylonians, who temporarily had lifted the siege (34:21). God was going to bring the Babylonians back, and they would destroy the city completely. The cities of Judah would become so desolate that no one could live in them (34:22).

C. Example of the Recabites (35:1–19)

1. *Testing of the loyalty of the Recabites* (35:1–11)

While Jehoiakim was still king of Judah, the Lord instructed Jeremiah to go to the "Recabites" ("Rechabites," KJV, JB, NAB, NEB, RSV) and invite them to one of the side rooms of the temple and give them wine to drink (35:1–2). The Recabites were descendants of the Kenites (1 Chron. 2:55; cf. Judg. 1:16). One of their most famous sons was Jonadab (also called Jehonadab), who joined Jehu in the blood purge of the family of Ahab, ca. 842 B.C. (2 Kings 10:15–27).

Jeremiah escorted them into the room of the sons of Hanan (35:4), set wine before them, and told them to drink it (35:5). Jeremiah was performing another of his symbolic acts by which he preached to Jeru-salem (see 13:1).

They refused to drink the wine, however, because their ancestor Jonadab had forbidden them to use it (35:6). Moreover, he had ordered that they live nomadic lives in tents, never settling in one place long enough to build houses or plant seeds or vineyards (35:7). Jonadab's motives are not known, but perhaps he saw the corruption and immorality in the cities and decided it was better for his family to live simple lives. That did not involve settling permanently in one location.

Whatever Jonadab's motives had been, his descendants 250 years later were still faithfully keeping his vows (35:8–10). They had only come into Jerusalem temporarily for protection from Nebuchadnezzar's armies that had come to punish Jehoiakim for his rebellion (35:11; cf. 2 Kings 24:1–2).

2. *Jeremiah's praise of the Recabites* (35:12–19)

The Lord instructed Jeremiah to go to the people of Jerusalem and ask them to profit from the Recabites' example (35:13–14). Jeremiah commended the Recabites for their faithful obedience to vows taken by an ancestor. By contrast, the descendants of the Israelites, who had made a covenant with God at Mount Sinai, refused to keep the vows imposed by that covenant. They refused to listen to God and had turned to their own wicked ways (35:15–16).

Because of their disregard for the vows of the covenant, God warned that He was going to bring disaster on them (35:17). By contrast, however, because of the faithfulness of the Recabites to the vows made by their ancestor, God pronounced a blessing on them. Their family would not become extinct but would always have someone to serve the Lord (35:19). The family did survive the destruction of Jerusalem, and one of its descendants is mentioned in Nehemiah 3:14.

D. Jehoiakim's Reaction to Jeremiah's Written Messages (36:1–32)

Chapter 36 is the only account in the Old Testament of how a prophet's words assumed written form. Most scholars believe that chapters 1–25 contain the messages that Jeremiah dictated in 36:32. Baruch recorded the messages on a "scroll" ("book," KJV), either papyrus or leather. We know Baruch did not use a book format, or codex, for this did not appear until the first or second century A.D.

1. *God's command to write the messages* (36:1–3)

In the year 605, the fourth year of Jehoiakim's reign and the twenty-third of Jeremiah's ministry, the Lord told Jeremiah to write down all that God had told him to speak since He first called him during Josiah's reign (36:2). In written form perhaps the messages would impress the people of Judah with the imminence of the calamity God was bringing on them and cause them to repent so He could forgive them (36:3).

2. *Dictation of the messages to Baruch* (36:4–7)

Jeremiah dictated the messages to his secretary Baruch from memory or from written notes he had kept. Baruch carefully copied them on a scroll (36:4). Jeremiah then commanded Baruch to take the writings to the temple on a certain day of fasting and read them to the crowd that would be present. Jeremiah was restricted at the time and could not read the messages himself (36:5–6). The nature of his restriction is not known. He may have been under arrest (although in 36:19 he was free to escape). He may have been banned by temple authorities from speaking in the precincts of the temple (cf. 20:1–6; 26:7–16).

3. *Reading the messages before the people* (36:8–10)

Baruch read the messages publicly almost a year later (36:9). The long delay from the time Jeremiah began dictating the messages is not explained. It did take some time for him to dictate all the messages; also it was necessary to wait until a designated day of fasting to read them. Baruch read the messages at the temple from the room of Gemariah, a son of Shaphan (36:10; cf. 26:24). The people's reaction to the messages is not recorded.

4. *Reading the messages before the officials* (36:11–19)

Micaiah, Gemariah's son, heard the words and immediately went to the palace and entered the secretary's room where all the officials were gathered (36:12). He related to them what he had heard when Baruch read the scroll (36:13). They were impressed and sent Jehudi (a descendant of Cushi and perhaps an Ethiopian) to Baruch to ask him to bring the scroll and read it to them (36:14). After listening to Baruch read the scroll again, they were frightened and insisted that the words be reported to the king (36:16).

They questioned Baruch as to how he came to write the scroll. He explained that Jeremiah had dictated the words to him, and he had copied them with ink (36:18; the only mention of this writing material in the Old Testament). The officials instructed Baruch that he and Jeremiah should hide themselves (36:19). They anticipated that in his rage upon hearing Jeremiah's words, King Jehoiakim might order the prophet's execution (cf. 26:20–23).

5. *Reading the messages before King Jehoiakim* (36:20–26)

After depositing the scroll in the room of Elishama the secretary for safekeeping, the officials went to the king and reported what they had just heard (36:20). Jehoiakim ordered Jehudi to bring the scroll and read it to him (36:21).

The text notes that these events were taking place in the ninth month (November–December). At that time the king was dwelling in his winter quarters. When the scroll was brought, a fire was burning in a firepot in the room (36:22). Jehoiakim showed no fear but only contempt for the messages. After hearing Jehudi read the contents of three or four columns of the scroll, the king would cut them off the scroll with a scribe's knife and throw them in the fire, repeating this procedure until the entire scroll was burned (36:23; cf. his father's attitude when he heard the word of the Lord, 2 Kings 22:11). By destroying the words, Jehoiakim probably believed he was nullifying their power. Even as he destroyed the scroll, Elnathan, Delaiah, and Gemariah (cf. 36:12) pleaded with him not to do so; but he would not listen (36:25).

Jehoiakim ordered a royal prince, Jerahmeel, together with Seraiah and Shelemiah, to arrest Baruch and Jeremiah; but "the LORD had hidden them" (36:26) until the king's wrath should subside.

6. *The rewriting of the scroll* (36:27–32)

Because Jehoiakim had rejected Jeremiah's written warnings that Nebuchadnezzar was coming to destroy Judah, the Lord pronounced judgment on him. He would have no heir to sit (the Hebrew word implies permanence) on the throne. (The temporary reign of three months by Jehoiachin does not conflict with this judgment.) Jehoiakim's corpse would be cast on the ground to endure the ravages of heat and cold (36:30; cf. 22:19; his body was probably exhumed and the bones scattered by the enemy when Jerusalem fell). He, his descendants, and his attendants would be punished for their sins, as well as all the people of Jerusalem and Judah (36:31).

Though we deplore Jehoiakim's contempt for the scroll, we can be grateful that because he destroyed it, we have even more of Jeremiah's messages. The Lord instructed Jeremiah to rewrite all the words that were on the first scroll; and when he did, he added other messages not included the first time (36:32). A scroll could be destroyed but not the living Word!

For Further Study

1. In a Bible dictionary or encyclopedia (see bibliography) read articles on: Lachish, slavery, Recabites, oaths, scroll, and scribe.

2. From a study of the biblical passages on slavery, determine what is God's attitude toward slavery.

3. Why does God take our vows and promises seriously?

4. What risk would you take to preserve God's written Word if you were ordered to destroy it?

PART THREE: *Messages in Time of National Crisis*

Chapter 9

The Siege and Fall of Jerusalem
(Jeremiah 37:1–40:6)

For forty years Jeremiah faithfully warned Judah of God's impending punishment if she did not repent. All warnings and pleas were ignored, so judgment came on the people who centuries before had been chosen to be "a kingdom of priests and a holy nation" (Exod. 19:6). Jeremiah 37–44 gives a detailed account of the siege and fall of Jerusalem and the aftermath of the events of 587. With the destruction of Jerusalem, Jeremiah was at last vindicated as a true prophet of God. Judah's tragedy was that, before the calamity, she had not believed he was a prophet.

A. Jeremiah's Imprisonment (37:1–21)

Jerusalem could not endure Jeremiah's dire predictions of disaster and his appeals to submit to Babylon. He was considered disloyal and a traitor to his own people. His theology that insisted the temple could be destroyed and the Davidic dynasty unseated was considered blasphemous. In order to keep him from further demoralizing the people and their will to resist, Jeremiah had to be silenced.

1. King Zedekiah's disobedience (37:1–2)

The events that were climaxed by the fall of Jerusalem occurred during the reign of Zedekiah, son of Josiah. Nebuchadnezzar had placed him on the throne of Judah when he deposed Coniah (Jehoiachin). Neither Zedekiah nor any of the people would listen to Jeremiah (37:1–2).

2. Prediction of a Babylonian victory (37:3–10)

Though the king would not heed Jeremiah's warnings, he must have sensed that Jeremiah was God's prophet. He sent Jehucal (spelled Jucal, 38:1) and Zephaniah (cf. 21:1) during the siege of Jerusalem to appeal to Jeremiah to pray to the Lord on Judah's behalf (37:3; cf. 21:1–2). Perhaps he thought the Lord would deliver Jerusalem now as He did in Hezekiah's time (2 Kings 19:35–36). Jeremiah had not yet been put in prison, though the city was under siege (37:4–5).

Zedekiah had probably been encouraged to rebel against Nebuchadnezzar (cf. 2 Chron. 36:13) by promise of military aid from Egypt. When the rebellion broke out, Nebuchadnezzar sent an army against Jerusalem to quell the revolt. Egypt made good its promise by sending an army to help the beleaguered city. However, when Nebuchadnezzar heard that the Egyptian army was approaching, he lifted the siege temporarily and pursued the hapless Egyptians back to Egypt (37:5–7). A hint of Nebuchadnezzar's activities at this time is found in Ezekiel 30:21, which suggests Egypt's defeat at his hands, and Ezekiel 29:7, which compares Egypt to a broken reed. Jeremiah sent word to Zedekiah that he should not conclude the danger was past because the siege had been lifted. The Babylonians were going to return, resume the siege, and destroy the city (37:8).

Jeremiah warned that the king should not deceive himself in thinking there was any hope. He said that even if Zedekiah defeated the entire Babylonian army, the surviving wounded soldiers would rally and destroy Jerusalem (37:10). There was no escape.

3. Jeremiah's arrest and imprisonment (37:11–15)

While Nebuchadnezzar was pursuing the Egyptian army, Jeremiah took advantage of the lifted siege to go take possession of some property in the land of Benjamin (37:12). We are not given any information about the transaction, but most scholars feel that the events of 32:1–15 supply the missing details. There we are told a kinsman requested Jeremiah to exercise the right of redemption and to buy his land in Anathoth that was about to be sold. During the lifting of the siege Jeremiah had his first opportunity to go examine the land he had purchased.

As he was leaving by the Benjamin Gate (perhaps in the north wall of the city), a guard named Irijah saw him departing. He arrested Jeremiah and accused him of deserting to the Babylonians (37:13; cf. 21:9). Jeremiah denied the charge, but it did no good. He was brought before officials who angrily had him beaten and then imprisoned in the house of Jonathan the secretary (37:15).

4. A secret interview with King Zedekiah (37:16–21)

Jeremiah was confined in a vaulted cell in an underground dungeon (37:16). Perhaps the other prisons were already filled, or they wanted to keep special watch over Jeremiah to prevent his escape. He remained imprisoned for some time until the king summoned him to the palace for a secret interview. Zedekiah asked if there was a word from the Lord. Jeremiah assured him there was, but it proved to be the same message he had already been preaching: Zedekiah would be taken prisoner by the victorious Nebuchadnezzar (37:17).

Then Jeremiah spoke in a mood reminiscent of some of his earlier "confessions," as when he complained about his mistreatment as the Lord's servant (e.g., 15:18). He asked what he had done to the king or his courtiers to deserve such abuse. He asked the king what had happened to the so-called prophets who said Nebuchadnezzar would not invade Judah (37:19). Events had proved that Jeremiah was right and the false prophets wrong. The barb was as close as Jeremiah ever came to saying, "I told you so." However, when we remember how much ridicule he had endured from his people, we may conclude that he deserved this one retort against the false prophets.

The treatment in Jonathan's house must have been intolerable, for Jeremiah, in a rare expression of self-concern, appealed to the king not to return him to Jonathan's house, lest he die there (37:20). The king granted the request and transferred Jeremiah to the courtyard of the guard where he remained until the day Jerusalem fell (37:21; cf. 38:28). Until the supply was exhausted, he was given an allotment of bread daily from the baker's street, so named because bakers located their shops there (37:21).

In his encounter with Jeremiah, Zedekiah emerges as a weak, vacillating king who wanted to believe Jeremiah and follow his advice. However, he did not have the courage to stand against his advisors. If he had followed Jeremiah's advice, even as late as the final weeks of siege, he could have prevented the burning of Jerusalem (38:17).

B. Jeremiah's Advice to Surrender (38:1–28)

1. Jeremiah's rescue from a cistern (38:1–13)

Shephatiah (otherwise unknown), Gedaliah (son of the Pashhur of 20:1 or 21:1, not the governor of 39:14), Jehucal (cf. 37:3), and Pashhur (cf. 21:1) heard Jeremiah appealing to the people to surrender to the

Babylonians in order to survive (38:1–2). They demanded that King Zedekiah order Jeremiah's death as he was discouraging (literally, "weakening the hands of") the soldiers and other inhabitants of Jerusalem. They were convinced that Jeremiah was not seeking their welfare but their ruin (38:4).

Zedekiah revealed his weak character by acceding to their demands. In a Pilate-like attempt to absolve himself of responsibility, he said, "He is in your hands. . . . The king can do nothing to oppose you" (38:5). Actually, however, Zedekiah could have opposed these men, for later he countermanded their deed by ordering Jeremiah's rescue when Ebed-Melech appealed to him, as the following narrative relates. The episode reveals how weak and spineless Zedekiah really was. He may have wanted to do the right thing, but he did not have the courage to do so.

Jeremiah was lowered by ropes into the cistern of the king's son "Malkijah" (38:6; "Malchiah," KJV). The cistern was located in the courtyard of the guard. The water in it had already been depleted, and so Jeremiah sank into the mud at the bottom and was left to die (38:6). The failure to kill Jeremiah outright may have resulted from a superstitious fear of killing a prophet.

A Cushite official ("Ethiopian eunuch," KJV) named Ebed-Melech (the name means "servant of the king") heard that Jeremiah had been placed in the cistern (38:7). He sought out the king, who was sitting in the Benjamin Gate (cf. 37:13), probably settling legal matters that were brought to him. Ebed-Melech accused the men of acting wickedly by placing Jeremiah in the cistern to die (38:9; the Hebrew says, "He is dead," meaning "He is as good as dead if he remains there"). Conscience stricken, Zedekiah gave orders to Ebed-Melech to take thirty men to assist him in removing Jeremiah from the pit (38:10). He may have thought that releasing Jeremiah would cause God to remove the Babylonian threat. Because thirty seems a large number for lifting one man from the cistern, the RSV, NAB, JB, and NEB (following one Hebrew manuscript) say there were three men. The large number can be explained, however, as necessary to avert any attempts by Jeremiah's adversaries to block his removal.

With tender concern for Jeremiah, the official used ropes to let down some old rags and worn-out clothes. He told Jeremiah to use the rags and clothes under his arms as pads so the ropes would not cut or bruise him as he was lifted from the pit. Jeremiah was then lifted from the cistern, and he remained in the courtyard of the guard (38:11–13).

2. *Jeremiah's final interview with King Zedekiah (38:14–28)*

King Zedekiah had Jeremiah brought to the third entrance to the temple (38:14). It perhaps was a royal entry (cf. 2 Kings 16:18). There the two men met for the last time before Jerusalem fell. Once again Zedekiah said he wanted to question Jeremiah and insisted that the prophet not hide anything from him (38:14). With good reason Jeremiah did not trust Zedekiah and was not eager to talk with him. He said, "If I give you an answer, will you not kill me?" (38:15). Jeremiah also must have felt it was useless to give any more advice to the king as he would not listen to him.

Zedekiah swore by a solemn oath, "As surely as the LORD lives" (cf. 4:2). He vowed that he would not kill Jeremiah or turn him over to those who wanted to kill him (38:16).

Reassured by the king's promise, Jeremiah told him again that the only way to save his life and to save the city was to surrender to the Babylonians (38:17). If this was not done, Jerusalem would be destroyed and Zedekiah would be taken prisoner (38:18).

Zedekiah expressed fear of the Jews who had gone over to the Babylonians. He was well aware that defeated kings were frequently tortured and horribly mutilated before being executed and was afraid he would be given to the Jews who had deserted to Nebuchadnezzar (38:19). Jeremiah assured Zedekiah that all would go well with him if he would obey the Lord (38:20).

However, to warn him about the consequences of not listening, Jeremiah described the horror that was coming on Jerusalem. The women left in the palace would be given to the Babylonian officials, and those same women would ridicule the king for allowing his trusted friends to mislead him. (In ancient times ridicule by a woman was the most humiliating experience a man could have; cf. Judg. 9:54). Jeremiah warned that Zedekiah's friends would desert him when his "feet are sunk in the mud" (38:22), a wordplay on Jeremiah's recent experience (38:6; cf. Obad. 7). The king's wives and sons would be taken prisoner as well as the king himself, and Jerusalem would be destroyed (38:23; the Hebrew says, "You will burn this city"). Zedekiah can be added to the list of Napoleons and Hitlers of history who sacrificed their people for their own vanity and selfish ambition.

As further evidence of his cowardice, Zedekiah warned Jeremiah not to reveal their conversation to anyone, lest he die (38:24). He anticipated that the officials would come and demand that Jeremiah tell them what he had said to the king. He instructed Jeremiah to reply that he had only presented a petition to the king asking not to be returned to Jonathan's house (38:26; cf. 37:15, 20).

Jeremiah departed from the courage and honesty we would have expected of him; when the officials questioned him, he answered just as the king had instructed him (38:27). Jeremiah's reply has been explained by some as an attempt to protect the city from a bloody purge. Others say he did it to save the life of Zedekiah from his own officials who might have killed him if they had thought he was being swayed by Jeremiah. Still others explain Jeremiah's acquiescence as a reminder that he was only human. He had preached for forty years, and no one listened to him. He had recently almost lost his life in a cistern for his truthfulness. For the moment he opted to avoid further confrontation.

Jeremiah was not the only man of God who deviated from the truth in time of stress (e.g., Abraham, Gen. 12:10–13; David, 1 Sam. 21:1–2; Peter, John 18:25–27). Such experiences remind us that all of us sin. Yet when we confess, God promises to forgive and He can continue to use us (1 John 1:9).

C. Capture of Jerusalem by the Babylonians (39:1–14)

1. *Fall of the city* (39:1–10)

Exact dates of events are not often found in the Bible, but the fall of Jerusalem was of such major significance that Jeremiah carefully recorded the day the siege began and the day the city fell. The siege began in the tenth month of the ninth year of Zedekiah's reign (39:1; i.e., December 589/January 588). Elsewhere we learn that it began on the tenth day of the month (52:4; 2 Kings 25:1; Ezek. 24:1). The city held out a year and a half until the food was gone (52:5–6); the people finally resorted to cannibalism (Lam. 4:10). The city walls were breached on the ninth day of the fourth month of the eleventh year of Zedekiah's reign (39:2; June/July 9, 587; cf. 52:6–7; 2 Kings 25: 3–4).

Babylonian officials triumphantly entered the devastated city and assembled at the Middle Gate (location unknown). They included

Nergal-Sharezer of Samgar, Nebo-Sarsekim (a chief officer), Nergal-Sharezer (a high official), and other officials (39:3).[1]

When Zedekiah and the remaining soldiers saw the Babylonians pouring through the breached walls, they fled by way of the king's garden by night through the gate between the two walls. They proceeded toward Jericho and in the direction of the Arabah ("the plain," KJV), that is, the region of the Jordan Valley down to the Gulf of Aqabah (39:4; cf. Ezek. 12:12–13).

The Babylonian army pursued them, however, and captured Zedekiah in the plains of Jericho. He was brought to Nebuchadnezzar's headquarters at Riblah in the land of Hamath (2 Kings 23:33). There the Babylonian monarch passed sentence on Zedekiah (39:5). He executed Zedekiah's sons before his eyes, killed the other nobles of Judah, and then put out Zedekiah's eyes, which was a common form of punishment. The king of Judah was led away in chains to Babylon (39:6–7). There he remained in prison till the day of his death (52:11).

The Babylonians systematically burned the royal palace and other houses and broke down the walls of Jerusalem (39:8). It is possible that these buildings, together with the temple, were burned a month after Jerusalem was taken (cf. 52:12–13). Nebuzaradan, commander of the imperial guard (literally, "chief of the slaughterers"), rounded up many of the people and took them to Babylon (39:9; cf. 52:29). He left some of the poorest people behind and gave them vineyards and fields to tend, as there would be no advantage to Nebuchadnezzar in leaving the land deserted (39:10; cf. 52:16).

2. *Liberation of Jeremiah* (39:11–14)

Nebuchadnezzar must have heard about Jeremiah's appeals to Jerusalem to surrender and insisted on rewarding the prophet. He gave instructions to Nebuzaradan to look after Jeremiah (literally, "set your eyes on him") and to do whatever he asked (39:12). So Nebuzaradan, together with some other officials, released Jeremiah from the courtyard where he had been detained during the siege (cf. 38:28; 40:1–6) and turned him over to Gedaliah (son of a friend named Ahikam; cf. 26:24). Thus Jeremiah was able to remain among his people in Judah (39:14).

---

[1]The reader is referred to the commentaries at the end of this book for further study of the problem of the proper names of the Babylonian officials. A check of translations shows six men (KJV, LXX), four men (RSV, NASB, TEV), three (NIV, NEB), and two (NAB, JB).

D. Promise of Deliverance to Ebed-Melech (39:15–18)

Even before Jerusalem fell, the Lord spoke to Jeremiah concerning Ebed-Melech while the prophet was still confined in the courtyard of the guardhouse. He wanted the Ethiopian to know that though the city would be taken, Ebed-Melech would not be captured or killed. His life would be spared ("as a prize of war," RSV) because he had trusted the Lord (39:17–18; cf. 45:5, where similar words were spoken to Baruch).

E. Release of Jeremiah (40:1–6)

These verses contain an account of Jeremiah's release after Jerusalem's fall that seems at first glance to be at variance with the narrative in 39:11–14. The first account said Nebuzaradan found Jeremiah in the courtyard of the guardhouse and released him (39:14), whereas this account says Jeremiah was taken in chains to Ramah, five miles north of Jerusalem, with other captives (40:1).[2] There Nebuzaradan found Jeremiah and told him that it was known to the Babylonians that Jeremiah's God had promised the disaster that came on Jerusalem for the sins of the people of Judah against their God (40:2–3). He freed Jeremiah and offered him the choice of remaining in his own land or of going to Babylon, where, undoubtedly, he would have been honored and taken care of the rest of his life (40:4).

Sensing Jeremiah's hesitation, Nebuzaradan encouraged him to remain with Gedaliah, who had been appointed governor over the cities of Judah. With these words he released Jeremiah and gave him provisions and a gift (40:5). Jeremiah journeyed to Mizpah. Its location is disputed, but it has been identified as Nebi Samwil, five miles north of Jerusalem or Tel en-Nasbeh, eight miles north of Jerusalem. At Mizpah he joined Gedaliah, being determined to remain among his own people and help in the long, arduous process of rebuilding (40:6). By remaining, Jeremiah silenced all accusations that he was a collaborator with the enemy and demonstrated his complete identification with his people in their tragedy.

---

[2]The two accounts can be harmonized, however. Jeremiah could have been released in Jerusalem and then picked up on the streets by soldiers who were rounding up people for deportation. He was taken with others in chains to Ramah where the mistake was discovered, and he was released again. Or perhaps Nebuzaradan made his headquarters in Ramah rather than devastated Jerusalem and had Jeremiah brought there, where he released him to Gedaliah.

For Further Study

1. In a Bible dictionary or encyclopedia (see bibliography) read articles on: Riblah and Ramah.

2. Make a list of all the people you can think of in the Bible who told a lie.

3. How can you account for Jeremiah's willingness to be untruthful when asked about the nature of his interview with Zedekiah?

4. If you had lived in Jerusalem during its siege, would you have thought Jeremiah was a traitor for calling on the city to surrender?

5. If you had been mistreated as Jeremiah was by his people, would you have accepted the offer to live in comfort in Babylon?

Chapter 10

Events After the Fall of Jerusalem and Words to Baruch

(Jeremiah 40:7–44:30; 45:1–5)

With Jerusalem's fall Jeremiah was vindicated as a prophet of God in the eyes of even his most ardent detractors. However, it was a hollow victory; and Jeremiah had no desire to gloat over the tragedy that had befallen his people, one that could have been averted had they listened to him. God having used him to "uproot," "tear down," "destroy," and "overthrow," he was ready to devote his efforts to the other part of his ministry—"to build and to plant" (1:10). Instead of going to Babylon, where he could have lived out his days in honor and ease, he remained with his people to do whatever he could to assist in the reconstruction of the nation.

A. The Governorship of Gedaliah (40:7–41:18)

1. The people's response to Gedaliah (40:7–12)

Angered by successive rebellions of Judah's last kings that required armed might to quell, Nebuchadnezzar determined that he would not appoint a successor to Zedekiah. Instead, he incorporated Judah into the empire as a province and named a native governor, Gedaliah, over those who remained there (40:7). Because Jerusalem was so thoroughly devastated, Gedaliah selected as the seat of government the city of Mizpah, where Judah's first king had been chosen (1 Sam. 10:17–25). A number of army officers and their men had escaped the Babylonian forces and were still in the open country. These officers came to Gedaliah, who assured them that they need not be afraid to serve their conquerors (40:8–9). He promised to represent them before the king. Then he ordered them to harvest the summer crops that had been neglected during the fighting (40:10).

Other Jews had fled to Moab, Ammon, Edom, and other lands. They began returning home on learning that Nebuchadnezzar had established a new government headed by one of their own people. They also joined in the harvesting of the crops (40:11–12).

2. *A warning to Gedaliah of a plot against his life* (40:13–16)

Some army officers led by Johanan came to Gedaliah to warn him of a plot against his life by Ishmael, who had been among the first who came to Gedaliah when he became governor (40:14; cf. 40:8). Gedaliah refused to believe them, but Johanan insisted and volunteered to kill Ishmael secretly. He feared that if Gedaliah were murdered worse vengeance would be heaped on the survivors by Nebuchadnezzar (40:15). Gedaliah was still unwilling to believe there was danger and accused Johanan of lying about Ishmael (40:16).

3. *The murder of Gedaliah* (41:1–3)

Ishmael, a member of the royal family, came in the seventh month with ten men to dine with Gedaliah (41:1). It might have been the same year of Jerusalem's fall, or several years later if the deportation of 582 reflects Nebuchadnezzar's revenge for Gedaliah's murder (cf. 52:30). While at the table Ishmael and his men arose and killed the unsuspecting governor along with Jews and Babylonians who were with him in Mizpah (41:2–3). His death was marked in later Judaism by a fast in the seventh month (cf. Zech. 7:5; 8:19).

Ishmael's motives for killing Gedaliah can only be surmised. Perhaps he considered Gedaliah a traitor who deserved to die. Or, since he was a member of the royal family, he may have been jealous of Gedaliah and felt the leadership should have gone to him. It has been suggested that his real purpose was to avenge himself on Nebuchadnezzar through his subordinates for deposing Zedekiah, or to weaken Babylonian authority any way he could. Perhaps his only motive for killing Gedaliah was that Baalis, the Ammonite king, had paid him to do so, thereby hoping to annex Judah to his own domains (cf. 40:14). Baalis had no desire to see Judah revitalized.

4. *Other violent acts of Ishmael* (41:4–10)

Whatever had motivated Ishmael to slay Gedaliah, he was not through with his slaughter. The next day, while his deed was yet undiscovered, eighty pilgrims came from Shechem, Shiloh, and

Samaria on their way to the ruined temple site in Jerusalem with grain offerings and incense. With their beards shaved off, their clothing torn, and their flesh cut as signs of mourning, they showed their grief over the fall of Jerusalem (41:5).

Ishmael went out from Mizpah to greet the pilgrims, feigning tears. He invited them in to see Gedaliah. However, as soon as they entered the city he slaughtered seventy of them and threw their bodies in a cistern that had been built by King Asa (41:6–7, 9). Ten of the pilgrims escaped death by offering food supplies they had hidden in a field for protection from plunder during a time of lawlessness (41:8). Perhaps Ishmael was trying to prevent word of the murder of Gedaliah getting out until he had time to escape, or he was simply seeking plunder.

Those who remained alive in Mizpah, including the king's daughters, were taken captive by Ishmael and forced to go with him toward Ammon, where he would be safe (41:10). Jeremiah was probably among the captives, though he is not mentioned.

5. Rescue of the captives (41:11–18)

Johanan and the other army officers heard what Ishmael had done and set out in pursuit of him. They overtook him at the great pool of Gibeon (41:11–12; cf. 2 Sam. 2:12–16). Ishmael was unable to hold his captives, who escaped and joined Johanan (41:14). Ishmael fled to Ammon with eight of his men (41:15).

Johanan and all those who were with him determined that they would flee to Egypt. They hoped that there they might escape the wrath of Nebuchadnezzar that they feared would descend on the whole land when he learned of Gedaliah's death (41:17–18).

B. The Flight to Egypt (42:1–43:7)

1. Jeremiah's advice sought (42:1–6)

Before they fled to Egypt, Johanan and those with him decided to seek Jeremiah's advice. For forty years no one had listened to Jeremiah, but finally he had become respected as a prophet of God.

They asked Jeremiah to pray to the Lord to tell them what to do (42:3). Jeremiah agreed to pray and to tell them whatever the Lord directed (42:4). They further assured Jeremiah that they would do whatever the Lord told them to do, whether it seemed good or bad (42:5–6). They probably secretly hoped Jeremiah would confirm what they had already decided to do.

2. God's answer (42:7–22)

Jeremiah waited ten days before receiving an answer from the Lord (42:7). He would not speak until he had a word from God. The message was essentially the same one he had preached before Jerusalem fell. The people were to stay in the land and not fear the king of Babylon. If they refused and fled to Egypt, sword, famine, and disease would pursue them to Egypt; and there they would die without survivors (42:10–17).

If they disobeyed, God's wrath would be poured out on them as it had been on Jerusalem (42:18). Jeremiah reminded them again that they had asked him to seek divine guidance and that they were only deceiving themselves if they disobeyed. Even as he spoke, Jeremiah must have known that the people would no more listen to him that day than they had in the past (42:20–22).

3. The people's response (43:1–7)

Judah had learned no lessons from the fall of Jerusalem. The people, though having irrefutable proof that Jeremiah was God's prophet, still refused to heed his advice. As soon as he finished speaking, they turned on him and accused him of lying. They denied that God had told him to advise them to remain in Judah (43:2).

Further, they charged that Baruch was inciting Jeremiah to speak as he did in order to see them killed or exiled by the Babylonians (43:3). It cannot be determined why they believed Baruch exercised influence over Jeremiah. Their attitude toward him, however, shows that he was more than just a secretary in Jeremiah's service. He must have been a person of influence in Judah. Jeremiah 45:5 suggests that Baruch was a man with personal ambition that had to be rebuked.

Johanan and the other army officers then led the people to Egypt, forcing Jeremiah and Baruch to go with them (43:5–6). They journeyed as far as Tahpanhes in Egypt (modern Tel Defneh in northeastern Egypt) before they halted and settled down (43:7; cf. 2:16).

C. Jeremiah in Egypt (43:8–44:30)

1. A symbolic act concerning Egypt's fate (43:8–13)

Though in Egypt against his will, Jeremiah continued to be God's prophet. The word of the Lord came to him in Tahpanhes, instructing him to perform a symbolic act. He was to take some large stones and bury them in clay in the brick pavement at the entrance to Pharaoh's palace in Tahpanhes in the presence of the Jews (43:9).

Then he was to tell them that God was bringing Nebuchadnezzar to Egypt ("my servant"; cf. comment at 25:9). He would set up his throne in a great victory celebration over Egypt on the very stones Jeremiah had buried there (43:10). It was useless to flee to Egypt, for Nebuchadnezzar would pursue them there. As a shepherd wraps his garment around him, so Nebuchadnezzar would wrap helpless Egypt around himself and depart safely after subjugating the land (43:11–12). Egypt would be devastated by the Babylonian conqueror. He would burn the temples of their gods and shatter the sacred pillar at Beth Shemesh (43:13; literally, "house of the sun," probably On, whose Greek name was Heliopolis). Nebuchadnezzar did invade Egypt in 568/7, but the extent of his conquest is not known.

2. *A rebuke of idolatry in Egypt* (44:1–14)

The Jews who first came to Tahpanhes were now living in various parts of Egypt, including Migdol, Memphis, and Upper Egypt (Hebrew, "Pathros"; consult a Bible dictionary for the location of these places). Jeremiah reminded them of the ruin that God had brought on Judah because of their sins (44:2–3). They had refused to listen to the prophets whom the Lord had sent again and again (44:4–5). He told his listeners that they were bringing similar calamity on themselves because of their idolatry (44:8; "what your hands have made"). Had they forgotten so soon the wickedness that brought the punishment God had inflicted on the nation (44:9)? Those who had fled to Egypt were not contrite; therefore, God determined to punish them in that land (44:10–12), even as He had punished Jerusalem (44:13). None of them would ever return to Judah, except for a few fugitives (44:14; cf. comment on 4:27).

3. *The people's scornful response* (44:15–19)

The Jews who heard Jeremiah's warnings said they would not listen to him (44:16). Rather, they determined that they would worship the Queen of Heaven, a fertility goddess (44:17; cf. comments on 7:18). They believed their calamity had come on them because they had stopped worshiping her (44:17–18). Their neglect of the Queen of Heaven probably began during Josiah's religious reforms (cf. 2 Kings

23:4–20). Husbands gave their consent for their wives to worship the Queen of Heaven (44:19; cf. Num. 30:10–15).

4. Further condemnation of the people (44:20–23)

Jeremiah rejected their interpretation of events. He insisted that God had not failed them. Rather, their abominable idolatry had brought ruin on Judah (44:23).

5. Jeremiah's last recorded words (44:24–30)

Jeremiah's patience with the exiles seemed to have come to an end. Since they were determined to worship the Queen of Heaven, he sarcastically said, "Go ahead then, do what you promised! Keep your vows" (44:25). However, he warned them that they could never again call on the name of the Lord for help (44:26). When judgment came, they would know whether their word or God's word would stand (44:28).

As a sign that Jeremiah's threat of punishment was true, he said Pharaoh Hophra would be given over to his enemies just as Zedekiah had been given to Nebuchadnezzar (44:29–30; cf. Isa. 7:14). Hophra was overthrown in 570 B.C., and succeeded by Amasis.

These are the last recorded words of Jeremiah. His fate is not known. Some think he returned to Judah; others think he eventually went to Babylon. It is more likely that he lived out his days in Egypt, warning and exhorting the disobedient people to return to the Lord. A legend persists that he was stoned to death by the Jews and that his body was later removed to Alexandria by Alexander the Great.

D. Words to Baruch (45:1–5)

No plausible reason can be given for Jeremiah's personal words to Baruch to be appended here rather than at the end of chapter 36. They were spoken after Baruch had copied Jeremiah's dictated messages on a scroll in 605 (45:1).

Equally uncertain are the circumstances that caused Jeremiah to speak to Baruch as he did. Baruch had been complaining that there was no rest from the sorrow and pain he felt (45:3). Perhaps he wanted to know what his reward would be for his faithful service and personal sacrifice. Through Jeremiah, the Lord warned Baruch not to seek great things for himself (45:5). The Lord was about to bring disaster on Judah, and it was no time to harbor personal ambition. The most

Baruch could expect would be to survive the coming calamity ("I will give you your life as a prize of war," RSV; cf. 39:18).

For Further Study

1. In a Bible dictionary or encyclopedia (see bibliography) read articles on: Ammon, Mizpah, Tahpanhes, and Hophra.

2. Was Gedaliah's refusal to suspect Ishmael a virtue or a defect in his character?

3. Why were the people of Judah still unwilling to believe Jeremiah even after his prophecies of Jerusalem's destruction were fulfilled?

4. Study chapter 45 carefully to see if you can determine the nature of Baruch's complaint.

PART FOUR: *Messages Against Foreign Nations*

Chapter 11

Judgment On the Nations
(Jeremiah 46:1–51:64)

Every prophetic book in the Old Testament with the exception of Hosea contains oracles directed against foreign nations. The major oracles are Amos 1–2, Isaiah 13–23, Zephaniah 2, Jeremiah 46–51, and Ezekiel 25–32.

Pronouncement of judgment on the nations should not be construed as an act of partiality for Israel or vindictiveness against others. God saw that the other nations were hopelessly corrupt; and, being righteous, He determined that they should be punished. History has proved that internal decadence is the chief cause of the fall of nations.

It is never stated that a prophet traveled to the nations he addressed and delivered the messages personally (except Jonah). His primary ministry was to Israel or Judah. Why, then, did so many of the prophets speak against other nations? Of course, an important purpose was to announce judgment on those nations. If God is Lord of the whole earth, He will have something to say about all nations. However, their messages were primarily intended to accomplish something among their Israelite audiences. Such messages would certainly have gotten the attention of the prophet's audiences when they heard judgment pronounced on their enemies (e.g., Amos 1–2). However, it would be demeaning to say these messages only served as attention getters.

Another purpose was to give comfort to God's people that He does not let evil go unpunished and that His people would eventually be delivered from wicked oppressors.

A final purpose of the messages was to warn Israel and Judah that they could not escape God's judgment. If nations were punished that did not claim to have a covenant relation with Him, how much more could the covenant people expect to be held accountable!

Though the messages against foreign nations comprise an extensive part of the Book of Jeremiah, they are usually given little attention by Bible students. They are about little-known people and places, whereas our primary interest is in Israel. Also, their vengeful spirit conflicts with the New Testament emphasis on love and forgiveness, and therefore they make us uncomfortable.

However, they contain important theological principles. They teach the universal sovereignty of God; no nation can escape His judgment. They teach that God can use one nation as an instrument of judgment on another. They imply that God's moral laws are universal, else the nations would not have been punished for breaking them. With their occasional word of hope, they teach that God cares for nations that are hostile to Him.

A. Introduction (46:1)

The opening statement has been generally interpreted as an introduction to all the messages of chapters 46–51. Some scholars have rejected all or part of these messages as authentic utterances of Jeremiah. However, since Jeremiah was called to be a prophet to the nations (1:5, 10), we should expect such messages from him.

The careful reader will observe that a similar pattern is followed in all these judgment speeches. First, a nation is singled out for judgment. Then a particular sin is usually named; most often it is pride. Next, punishment is pronounced, which in every case is defeat by an enemy. Finally, the nation that will be used as the instrument of judgment is usually, but not always, named. Most frequently that nation is Babylon. A word of hope after judgment is added for four of the nations—Egypt (46:26), Moab (48:47), Ammon (49:6), and Elam (49:39).

B. Judgment on Egypt (46:2–28)

1. *Egyptian defeat at Carchemish* (46:2–12)

With vivid word pictures Jeremiah described the defeat of Egypt by Babylon at the battle of Carchemish in 605 (46:2–6). The battle was significant, for it determined that Babylon had emerged as the undisputed principal power in the ancient world. It was also a day of vengeance for the Lord (46:10). There would be no healing for virgin Egypt's wound (46:11; cf. 14:17).

2. *The coming of Nebuchadnezzar* (46:13–26)

Jeremiah named Nebuchadnezzar as the one who would smite Egypt (46:13). Pharaoh would be ridiculed as "only a loud noise" (46:17). Egypt was compared to a beautiful heifer against whom a "gadfly" ("horsefly," NASB; "destruction," KJV) was coming from the north to sting (46:20). Her mercenaries were fatted calves that would flee from the enemy (46:21). Her people would hiss helplessly like a fleeing serpent before the advancing enemy (46:22). Punishment would include her gods and Pharaoh himself (46:25), but afterward Egypt would be inhabited as in the past (46:26; cf. Ezek. 29:13–16).

3. *Words of assurance to Israel* (46:27–28)

Lest Jacob, "my servant" (46:27; cf. Isa. 44:1–2) be dismayed, the Lord assured His covenant people that though He was going to punish them, He would bring them back from the nations where they had been scattered and destroy those nations that had afflicted them (46:27–28; cf. 30:10–11).

C. Judgment on the Philistines (47:1–7)

Jeremiah's message against the Philistines was spoken before Pharaoh attacked Gaza (either 609 before the battle of Megiddo or 605 after his defeat at Carchemish). No particular sin was singled out, but the enemy would come like a flood from the north (47:2) as God's agent of destruction (47:4). Terrorized, the Philistines would even abandon their own children (47:3). The "sword of the LORD" would not rest until God's vengeance was complete on Israel's ancient enemy (47:6).

D. Judgment on Moab (48:1–47)

The messages against Moab are disproportionately long when compared to her political importance and influence on Israel. Mention of a large number of place names, many unknown, is an unusual feature of these messages.

1. *The destruction of Moab* (48:1–10)

The cities of Moab, including "Madmen" (48:2; from a Hebrew word "be silent" or "dung") were all going to be destroyed. No one would escape, not even her god Chemosh (48:7–8). Moab's sin was pride in her accomplishments and in her wealth (48:7; cf. 48:29).

2. *The shame of Moab* (48:11-20)

Moab had not known trouble for many years. She was like wine whose sediment sinks to the bottom of the container and remains undisturbed (48:11). But she would be poured out and then smashed like a jar (48:12). The agent of destruction is not named but is called a destroyer (48:8, 18, 32) and a swooping eagle (48:40). Babylon was probably intended.

3. *Judgment on the cities of Moab* (48:21-27)

The Lord pronounced judgment on the cities of Moab, calling them by name (48:21-24). Moab would be like a horn cut off, a broken arm (48:25), and a drunkard wallowing in his vomit (48:26; cf. Prov. 26:11; Isa. 19:14). Moab had ridiculed Israel but was now going to become a laughingstock herself (48:26-27).

4. *The pride of Moab* (48:28-33)

Moab's pride and arrogance were well-known (48:29), but her insolence and boasting would be silenced (48:30). There would be weeping for Moab (48:31-32) over the devastation of the fruitful land. Shouts of joy would no longer be heard (48:33).

5. *Lament over Moab* (48:34-39)

The Lord was determined to put an end to Moab's idolatry (48:35). There would be wailing (48:36), and the people would display symbols of grief, including baldness, cutting the flesh, and wearing of sackcloth (48:37). There would be lamentation everywhere for the shattered vessel (48:38-39).

6. *Captivity and restoration of Moab* (48:40-47)

Moab would suffer like a woman in labor (48:41) and cease to be a nation because of her arrogance toward the Lord (48:42). Her people would be taken captive (48:46); yet God would restore her fortunes in the latter days (48:47). No reason is given for God's mercy on Moab, but her judgment and future restoration parallel that of Israel.

E. **Judgment on Ammon** (49:1-6)

Ammon was to be punished because she had taken possession of the cities of Gad (49:1). She boasted of her fruitful land and riches and felt secure from attack (49:4). But the battle cry was going to be heard in the land, and her cities would be destroyed (49:2–3). Priest, princes, people, and even their god "Molech" (Hebrew, *malkam;* "their king," KJV) would be carried away captive by the unnamed enemy (49:3, 5). However, as with Moab, God would restore the fortunes of the Ammonites (49:6; cf. 48:47).

F. Judgment on Edom (49:7–22)

The Edomites were descendants of Esau (Gen. 36:1). They had been traditional enemies of Israel from the time of the conflict between the twin brothers, Esau and Jacob. Unlike the grape picker who leaves a few grapes on the vine or the thief who leaves a few possessions in the house (49:9), God was going to strip Edom bare (49:10; cf. Obad. 5–6). She would drink the cup of wrath (49:12; cf. 25:21). God had sworn by Himself (the most solemn oath that could be taken) that He would destroy the nation completely (49:13).

Because of their inaccessible location to enemies, the Edomites were proud (49:16; cf. Obad. 3–4). However, God was going to bring Edom down from her eagle's nest (49:16) and overthrow her cities like Sodom and Gomorrah (49:17–18). The enemy that would destroy Edom is not named, but Babylon is suggested in the descriptions as "like a lion coming up from Jordan's thickets" (49:19) and an eagle that swoops down (49:22; cf. Ezek. 17:2–6).

G. Judgment on Damascus (49:23–27)

No sin of this city is named, but its people were enemies of Israel. Damascus, a city of renown, would agonize like a woman in labor, and her streets would be filled with the corpses of her soldiers (49:24–26).

H. Judgment on Kedar and Hazor (49:28–33)

Kedar was a prosperous Arab tribe (cf. Gen. 25:13); and Hazor was an Arab town, tribe, or geographical region whose identification is otherwise uncertain. Their wealth had made them self-sufficient (49:31), but Nebuchadnezzar (49:28, 30) was going to plunder and destroy them (49:32–33). Hazor would remain desolate forever (49:33). Kedar and Hazor may have been included to show that not even an insignificant people can escape God's judgment.

I. Judgment on Elam (49:34–39)

Elam was located in the hill country east of Babylonia; its capital was

Susa. It is uncertain why a nation so far from Judah would be included as an object of judgment except to teach that God's power was unlimited and could reach faraway nations. No sin is singled out for mention in Jeremiah's only dated message against other nations (49:34). A coalition of many nations (49:36) would conquer Elam (49:37). However, the Lord declared that He would restore the fortunes of Elam in the last days (49:39).

J. Judgment on Babylon (50:1–51:64)

The message against Babylon is the longest of Jeremiah's oracles against foreign nations and the one that is most frequently denied to Jeremiah by many scholars. Though Babylon had been used as God's instrument of judgment on other nations, including Judah, and Nebuchadnezzar was called "my servant" (25:9), she would not escape God's judgment for her own sins (cf. 25:12).

The oracles against Babylon alternate the theme of Babylon's doom with promises of deliverance for Judah. There is no contradiction between Jeremiah calling for Judah to submit to Babylon and then condemning Babylon, as some scholars have contended (cf. 51:56; Isa. 10:5–27; 37:22–29; Hab. 1:6, 12–13; 2:6–8).

1. *Destruction of Babylon by a coalition of nations* (50:1–20)

Jeremiah has been denied as the author of these verses because they describe fallen Babylon and the disgrace of her powerless god Bel (50:2; also called "Merodach," but better known as "Marduk"). Babylon fell to the Persians in 539 B.C., long after Jeremiah's time. However, prophets frequently spoke of future events as though they had already happened (e.g., Amos 5:2). If God said it would happen, it was as good as done.

The invasion of Babylon would be led by a coalition of nations from the north (50:3, 9, 41; cf. 3:18; 4:6 et al., where Babylon was the enemy from the north). The sons of Israel and Judah would begin their journey home from exile (50:4–5) following the plunder and destruction of Babylon (50:10).

Babylon had exulted in her pillage of Judah (50:11). However, she was going to become a desolation (50:12–13; cf. 18:16; 19:8; 49:17), for by attacking Judah she was sinning against the Lord (50:14). Now the enemy would do to her as she had done to others (50:15). Israel had been scattered like sheep by Assyria, who in turn was punished. Now

Babylon was going to be punished in the same manner (50:17–18). God would then bring His sheep back to their land and pardon their sins (50:19–20).

2. The time of punishment is near (50:21–28)

The hammer that had pounded other nations to submission was about to be broken and caught in a trap because she dared oppose the Lord (50:23–24; cf. Isa. 10:5 concerning Assyria). The time of punishment has come. God would avenge the destruction of His temple (50:27–28; cf. 51:11).

3. A renewed call for the destruction of Babylon (50:29–46)

There would be no escape for the Babylonians because of their arrogance against the Holy One of Israel (50:29–32). God as Redeemer (cf. comment on 31:11) was going to be the advocate for His oppressed people (50:33–34). Sword and drought (words with the same consonants in Hebrew) would ravage the idolatrous land, making the false prophets of Babylon appear foolish (50:35–38). Wild animals would inhabit the desolated city (50:39). It would become uninhabited like Sodom and Gomorrah (50:40). The nation that had terrorized others would be seized by panic when its enemy came like a lion (50:41–44; cf. 49:19). When word went out that mighty Babylon had been captured, the nations of the earth would tremble (50:46; cf. 50:44–46 with 49:19–21, where almost identical words are used against Edom).

4. God's power will bring about Babylon's downfall (51:1–19)

God announced that He would raise up foreigners against Leb Kamai ("the midst of them that rise up against me," KJV).[1] These enemies would devastate her land (51:1–4). He then assured Israel and Judah that, though they were guilty, He would not forsake them (51:5).

Babylon was like a "gold cup," but she was under God's control (51:7; cf. Isa. 51:17, 23; Rev. 18:3). The "gold cup" may be a reference to her power and splendor, or it may mean the cup of wrath (cf. 25:15–16). The nations had drunk of her wine and had gone mad (51:7). She who was once God's cup of wrath was herself going to be smashed. There was no healing for Babylon (51:9) because God had determined

---

[1]Leb Kamai is an athbash (see explanation at 25:26) for the Chaldeans (the consonants *ksdym* become *lbqmy*), i.e., Babylonians. It means "the heart of those who rise up against me."

to destroy her (51:11). The enemy is identified for the first time as the Medes (51:11). The army of Cyrus, king of the Medes and Persians, was going to swarm over Babylon like locusts amid shouts of victory (51:14). In verses 15–19 the prophet repeated the hymn praising God that is also found in 10:12–16 (see comments there).

5. Babylon cannot stand against God (51:20–44)

The nation God has used as his "war club" (literally, a "shatterer") and who has been a destroying mountain will become useless like a burned-out mountain and will be desolate forever (51:20–26). Some scholars understand verses 20–23 as words addressed to Cyrus, the coming conqueror of Babylon, rather than to Babylon.

In His capacity as leader of the forces being assembled against Babylon, the Lord ordered the blowing of the trumpet to call the nations together (51:27–28). In the day of destruction the strength of the Babylonian soldiers will be exhausted, and they will become like women (51:30). Messengers will report to the king of Babylon that the city has been taken (51:31; cf. 2 Sam. 18:19–33). Babylon will be like a threshing floor that has been trodden down to make it smooth and hard at the beginning of harvest (51:33).

The time will come when the inhabitants of Zion will say that Nebuchadnezzar has devoured them like a "serpent" (51:34; "monster," NASB; "dragon," KJV; cf. Jonah 1:17). They will call for blood vengeance (51:35), and God will hear their pleas (51:36). He will make Babylon a desolated ruin and a habitation of wild animals (51:37). Their shouts like the lion roaring over its prey and their laughter will be silenced like a drunkard who goes to sleep and never awakes (51:38–39). God will bring them down like lambs to the slaughter (51:40).

Sheshak (cf. 25:26 for explanation of this name for Babylon) will be engulfed like waves from the sea (51:41–42) and made an uninhabitable land (51:43). Bel (see comment on 50:2) will be punished and forced to disgorge his victims (51:44). Pilgrims will no longer stream to his shrine, for even the walls of the city will fall (51:44).

6. Another warning of Babylon's destruction (51:45–58)

Babylon will fall to an enemy from the north (51:48) because of Israel's slain and the disgrace she brought to Jerusalem by desecrating the temple (51:49–51). The idols of Babylon will be punished. She cannot escape God's destroyers even if she should fortify a place in heaven against them (51:52–53). There will be a great outcry in Babylon when the Lord repays her for her evil (51:54). Her mighty men will sleep forever, and her walls and gates will be destroyed by the enemy that will sweep over her like a tidal wave (51:55–58).[2]

7. *Jeremiah's message cast into the Euphrates* (51:59–64)

Jeremiah learned that Seraiah, brother of Baruch and a "staff officer" ("quiet prince," KJV), was accompanying Zedekiah to Babylon in 594/3 (51:59; cf. 32:12). The occasion for Zedekiah's visit to Nebuchadnezzar is not given, but he was probably summoned by the monarch to reaffirm his loyalty (cf. 27:3, which may refer to an intended rebellion of nations led by Zedekiah, and 2 Chron. 36:13). There is no reason to question the historicity of the visit, as some scholars have done.

Jeremiah wrote messages of judgment against Babylon on a scroll (51:60) and asked Seraiah to take the scroll with him and to read it aloud when he arrived in Babylon (51:61–62). Then he was to tie a stone to the scroll and to toss it into the Euphrates River (51:63). We are not told whether the audience that actually witnessed this symbolic act was large or small; however, its meaning was clear. Just as the weighted scroll would sink to the bottom of the river, Babylon was going to sink, never to rise again, because of the disaster God was going to bring on her (51:64).

It is of interest to observe that the Hebrew text of 1:1 begins with "the words of Jeremiah," and 51:64 ends with the same phrase. There is little doubt that it was deliberately inserted in both places to unify the book from first to last.

For Further Study

1. Using an up-to-date atlas or Bible dictionary locate and study the geographical place names in chapters 46–51 with which you are not familiar.

2. What lessons can be learned from the messages against the foreign nations?

---

[2]Babylon's walls were one of the wonders of the ancient world. They were composed of outer and inner walls for the security of the city. They were between 11–25 feet wide and perhaps 40–60 feet high.

PART FIVE: *A Historical Postscript*

Chapter 12

A Summary of Events From Zedekiah's Reign to Jehoiachin's Release

(Jeremiah 52:1–34)

The closing chapter of the Book of Jeremiah is essentially a repetition of 2 Kings 24:18–25:30, omitting 2 Kings 25:22–26 (cf. Isa. 36–39 with 2 Kings 18:13–20:19, where events of Hezekiah's reign are recorded in both places). The narrative of 2 Kings was probably added here to emphasize the fact that Jeremiah's prophecies had been fulfilled.

The most important addition to Jeremiah 52 not found in 2 Kings is the listing of the number of people carried away in each of three deportations (52:28–30). It reveals that the number of exiles was relatively small and was probably composed of carefully chosen people. The exiles included members of the royal family and political prisoners who, if left behind, might rally the survivors to rise up in rebellion again. They also included skilled craftsmen who could be useful to Nebuchadnezzar. Their departure symbolized the total defeat of the covenant people, but these same people became the nucleus of the remnant that would return one day to rebuild the land.

A. The Reign of King Zedekiah (52:1–11)

These verses summarize the reign of Zedekiah, who became king at age twenty-one after the rebellion that began in 598 had been quelled. They briefly describe the siege of Jerusalem that lasted a year and a half before the city fell (cf. 39:1–10). They conclude with the capture and fate of the king who could have saved Jerusalem if he had listened to Jeremiah (52:11).

B. The Destruction of Jerusalem (52:12–27)

This passage summarizes the systematic destruction of Jerusalem that was supervised by Nebuzaradan, commander of the imperial guard. It is noted that some of the poorest were carried away into exile (52:15) and that some of the poor were left behind to cultivate the land (52:16; cf. 39:10). The temple was looted; some of the temple furnishings and treasures, including the huge bronze Sea described extensively in 1 Kings 7, were broken up so their bronze could be carried to Babylon (52:17). Ritual implements of gold, silver, and bronze were carried away intact as trophies of war (52:18–23).

Among those taken captive was Seraiah, the chief priest (52:24; not Seraiah, Baruch's brother, 51:59; cf. 1 Chron. 6:14; Ezra 7:1). The captives also included certain other priests, officials, and the officer in charge of conscripting the "people of the land" (52:25; a term that sometimes refers to the general population, but at other times refers to landowners). They were brought to Nebuchadnezzar at Riblah and executed (52:26–27).

C. The Three Deportations of the People (52:28–30)

In 597 ("the seventh year," i.e., of Nebuchadnezzar's reign; but cf. 2 Kings 24:12) after successfully putting down Jehoiakim's revolt, Nebuchadnezzar carried 3,023 of the Jews into exile (52:28). These included Jehoiachin (2 Kings 24:15) and Ezekiel (Ezek. 1:1–3). There is no conflict with 2 Kings 24:14, which says ten thousand were taken. The smaller figure counted adult males only, whereas the larger number included women and children who were also taken.[1]

After the destruction of Jerusalem in 587 (the eighteenth year of Nebuchadnezzar's reign), the Babylonian monarch took 832 into exile (52:29). They were clearly leaders and other key people.

In 582 (the twenty-third year of Nebuchadnezzar's reign) a third deportation took place that involved 745 people (52:30). The cause for this third deportation is not known. Some believe it may have been Nebuchadnezzar's vengeance for Gedaliah's murder (41:1–3). It was undoubtedly punishment for some act of insurrection. Altogether in the three deportations 4,600 people were taken.

---

[1]Another view is that 52:28–30 is not an exhaustive list of the deportations but rather a statement of deportations not recorded elsewhere. The deportation of the 3,023 Jews that took place in Nebuchadnezzar's "seventh year" (Jer. 52:28) is understood to coincide with the capture and death of Jehoiakim, who rebelled. Its purpose was to warn the Jews not to rebel again. However, there was further rebellion under Jehoiakim's son Jehoiachin; and so Nebuchadnezzar came again in his "eighth year" (2 Kings 24:12) and carried away more than 10,000 people. This view is discussed by Theo. Laetsch, *Bible Commentary: Jeremiah* (Saint Louis: Concordia Publishing House, 1952), p. 370.

D. Release of King Jehoiachin From Prison (52:31–34)

The book closes with the account of Jehoiachin's release after thirty-seven years of imprisonment (cf. 2 Kings which closes with the same narrative, 25:27–30). Jeremiah was not likely alive when this event took place. Jehoiachin was released in 561 B.C. by Nebuchadnezzar's successor, Evil-Merodach (Amel-Marduk in the Babylonian language), and given special honor by the king the rest of his days (52:31–34). Captured kings were frequently kept at the conqueror's court as trophies of his military triumphs. Babylonian records have been found that say Jehoiachin and his sons received monthly rations of oil.

The inclusion of Jehoiachin's release as the final word in the Book of Jeremiah served as a slight glimmer of hope to the downtrodden covenant people that perhaps a day would come when all of them would be released from their subjugation.

For Further Study

1. Why do you think 2 Kings 24:18–25:30 were repeated as the closing words of the Book of Jeremiah?

2. See if you can review from memory the principal events in the life and ministry of Jeremiah.

Bibliography

Commentaries on Jeremiah

Blackwood, Andrew W., Jr. *Commentary on Jeremiah.* Waco, Texas: Word Books, Publisher, 1977.

Bright, John. *Jeremiah: Introduction, Translation, and Notes.* The Anchor Bible, vol. 21. Garden City, New York: Doubleday & Co., Inc., 1965.

Harrison, R. K. *Jeremiah and Lamentations: An Introduction and Commentary.* Tyndale Old Testament Commentaries. London: The Tyndale Press, 1973.

Hyatt, James Philip. "The Book of Jeremiah: Introduction and Exegesis." In *The Interpreter's Bible,* vol. 5, pp. 777-1142. Edited by George Arthur Buttrick et al. New York/Nashville: Abingdon Press, 1956.

Keil, C. F. *The Prophecies of Jeremiah.* Translated from the German by James Kennedy. Biblical Commentary on the Old Testament, 2 vols. Grand Rapids: William B. Eerdmans Publishing Co., 1956 reprint.

Kuist, Howard Tillman. *The Book of Jeremiah. The Lamentations of Jeremiah.* The Layman's Bible Commentary, vol. 12. Richmond: John Knox Press, 1960.

Laetsch, Theo. *Bible Commentary: Jeremiah.* Saint Louis: Concordia Publishing House, 1952.

Leslie, Elmer A. *Jeremiah: Chronologically Arranged, Translated, and Interpreted.* New York/Nashville: Abingdon Press, 1954.

Morgan, George Campbell. *Studies in the Prophecy of Jeremiah.* London: Oliphants, 1963.

Nicholson, E.W. *Jeremiah 1-25.* The Cambridge Bible Commentary on the New English Bible. Cambridge: University Press, 1973.
_____. *Jeremiah 26-52.* The Cambridge Bible Commentary on the New English Bible. Cambridge: University Press, 1975.

Orelli, C. von. *The Prophecies of Jeremiah.* Edinburgh: T. & T. Clark, 1889.

Peake, Arthur Samuel. *Jeremiah and Lamentations.* Century Bible, 2 vols. Edinburgh: T. C. and E. C. Jack, 1910-1911.

Streane, A. W. *The Book of the Prophet Jeremiah together with the Lamentations.* The Cambridge Bible for Schools and Colleges. Cambridge: University Press, 1892.

Thompson, J. A. *The Book of Jeremiah.* The New International Commentary on the Old Testament. William B. Eerdmans Publishing Co., 1980.

Bible Dictionaries and Encyclopedias

Buttrick, George Arthur, ed. *The Interpreter's Dictionary of the Bible.* 4 vols. New York/Nashville: Abingdon Press, 1962.

Crim, Keith, ed. *The Interpreter's Dictionary of the Bible: Supplementary Volume.* Nashville: Abingdon Press, 1976.

Douglas, J. D., ed. *The New Bible Dictionary.* Grand Rapids: William B. Eerdmans Publishing Co., 1970.

Orr, James, ed. *The International Standard Bible Encyclopedia.* 5 vols. William B. Eerdmans Publishing Co., 1957 reprint.

Tenney, Merrill C., ed. *The Zondervan Pictorial Bible Dictionary.* Rev. ed. Grand Rapids: Zondervan Publishing House, 1967.
_____. *The Zondervan Pictorial Encyclopedia of the Bible.* 5 vols. Grand Rapids: Zondervan Publishing House, 1975.

Unger, Merrill F. *Unger's Bible Dictionary.* Chicago: Moody Press, 1957.

Bible Translations

Good News Bible: The Bible in Today's English Version. New York: American Bible Society, 1976. (Referred to in the Study Guide as TEV.)

Jerusalem Bible. Garden City, New York: Doubleday & Co., Inc., 1966. (Referred to in the Study Guide as JB.)

King James Version. (Referred to in the Study Guide as KJV.)

Moffatt, James. *The Bible: A New Translation.* New York: Harper & Row, Publishers, 1954. (Referred to in the Study Guide as *Moffatt.*)

New American Bible. New York: The World Publishing Co., 1970. (Referred to in the Study Guide as NAB.)

New American Standard Bible. LaHabra, Cal.: Foundation Press Publications, 1973. (Referred to in the Study Guide as NASB.)

New English Bible. Oxford: Oxford University Press, 1970. (Referred to in the Study Guide as NEB.)

New International Version. Grand Rapids: Zondervan Bible Publishers, 1978. (Referred to in the Study Guide as NIV.)

Revised Standard Version. New York: Thomas Nelson & Sons, 1953. (Referred to in the Study Guide as RSV.)

Septuagint Version of the Old Testament and Apocrypha. Grand Rapids: Zondervan Publishing House, 1972 reprint. (Referred to in the Study Guide as LXX.)